FLY FISHING
for Beginners

by Chris Hansen

CREATIVE
PUBLISHING
international

CHANHASSEN, MINNESOTA

www.creativepub.com

© Sean Spraungle

CHRIS HANSEN is the manager of a retail fly-fishing store in Minneapolis, Minnesota, and has extensive experience teaching beginners how to fly fish. He organizes and conducts fly-casting and fly-tying classes and spends many days each spring, summer, and fall guiding novice fly anglers in the Midwest; he also spent two summers guiding in Alaska. Each winter Chris travels to places such as Texas, Florida, Mexico, and Belize to fly fish for various saltwater species.

CREATIVE PUBLISHING international

President/CEO: Michael Eleftheriou
Vice President/Publisher: Linda Ball

FLY FISHING FOR BEGINNERS
  By Chris Hansen
Executive Editor, Outdoor Products Group: Barbara Harold
Creative Director: Bradley Springer
Photo Editor: Angela Hartwell
Director, Production Services: Kim Gerber
Production Manager: Helga Thielen
Production Staff: Stephanie Barakos, Laura Hokkanen
Staff Photographer: Tate Carlson
Fish ID Illustrator: Joseph R. Tomelleri
Cover Photo: Brian O'Keefe
Contributing Photographers: Bill Beatty, Denver Bryan, Ted Fauceglia,
  Bill Buckley/The Green Agency, Victor Colvard/The Green Agency, Bill
  Lindner Photography, Brian O'Keefe, Steve Probasco,
  Jim Schollmeyer, Dusan Smetana, Neale Streeks
Contributing Manufacturers:
Abel Quality Products: p. 16BR
  165 Aviador Street/Camarillo, CA 93010
  tel: 805-484-8789/fax: 805-482-0701/www.abelreels.com
Action Optics: p. 47
  280 Northwood Way/Ketchum, ID 83340-2999
  tel: 800-654-6428/fax: 208-727-6576/www.actionoptics.com
Cortland Line Company: pp. 16TL, 16TR, 37T, 38B
  3736 Kellogg Road/Cortland, NY 13045-5588
  tel: 607-756-2851/fax: 607-753-8835/www.cortlandline.com
Loon Outdoors: 38R
  7737 West Mossy Cup St./Boise, ID 83709
  tel: 208-362-4437/fax: 208-362-4497/www.loonoutdoors.com
The Morell Company: 38T
  436 Webster Street/Needham Heights, MA 02494
  tel: 781-455-6905/fax: 781-453-8008
Redington: p. 16CR
  2589 SE Federal Highway/Stuart, FL 34997-7959
  tel: 800-253-2538/fax: 772-220-9957/www.redington.com
Ross Reels: p. 16BL
  1 Ponderosa Court/Montrose, CO 81401
  tel: 970-249-1212/fax: 970-249-1834/www.rossreels.com
Scientific Anglers: 16CL, 38C
  3M Center Building 223-2N-01/St. Paul, MN 55144-1000
  tel: 651-733-0591/fax: 651-737-7429/www.scientificanglers.com

Printing: R. R. Donnelley
  10 9 8 7 6 5 4 3 2 1

Library of Congress Cataloging-in-Publication Data
ISBN 1-58923-067-1

TABLE OF CONTENTS

Introduction...4

Fly Fishing Equipment...6

Casting a Fly...60

Catching Fish on Flies...72

Afterword...136

Introduction

In my opinion, to be a really good angler, you should be proficient with all types of sport fishing equipment: spinning, casting, and fly. I fish for all kinds of fish in all kinds of ways. But it was fly fishing for trout that really started my love of fishing, and after 25 years I still love it.

Almost every angler catches his or her first fish on some kind of live bait. What else are you going to give a five-year-old to fish with? Hang a worm under a bobber, cast it off the dock, reel in a sunny when the bobber goes down. There's hardly anything in the world that could be more of a sure thing. Using live bait takes a lot of variables out of the equation. But fly fishing adds some of the excitement back in!

This book is designed for people who have become proficient with spinning and casting tackle and are looking to expand their horizons, as well as for people who have fished very little, if at all, and are intrigued by the world of fly fishing. I hope that reading this book will answer many of your questions about fly fishing.

Read all you can, watch videos, ask questions of people you know who fly fish or fly shop employees—but above all else, to really learn about fly fishing, you must go fishing yourself.

You'll notice that I don't dwell too much on the flies themselves. There have already been countless books and magazine articles devoted strictly to that topic. In this book I will spend more time discussing fishing techniques. By using a reasonable fly with basic skills, you'll start catching fish right away. You can decide for yourself which flies work best for you.

Here are what I consider the eight most important things to remember, wherever you're fishing, and whatever you're fishing for. If you apply them every time you go out on the lake or stream, you're sure to catch fish!

1. Fish where the fish are. This may seem obvious, but it doesn't matter what fly you're using if there are no fish in the area.

2. Be able to cast a fly there. Good casting skills should be first learned on the lawn, and then honed on the stream.

3. Keep your fly wet. Go fishing as often as you can, and make the most of your time while you're out there.

4. Pay attention. Keep your eyes and ears open while on the water—notice rising fish, insects or baitfish the fish may feed on, and exactly where a fish was when it ate your fly.

5. Set the hook. To catch a fish, the hook must penetrate the fish's mouth. If you think that there's even a chance that a fish just ate your fly, set the hook.

6. Ask questions. Almost anyone who fly fishes loves to talk about it—your friends, people working in fly shops, people you meet on the stream or lake. Just ask.

7. Have confidence. It's hard to have confidence when doing something new. But if you have basic casting skills, use a reasonable fly, and keep it wet, you should EXPECT to catch a fish. And after you catch that first fish, the next one will be much easier.

8. Have fun. Even on days when things aren't going right, you can have fun!

With the information in this book—and lots of practice—you'll become a successful fly angler, and have lots of fun catching all kinds of fish!

Fly Fishing
EQUIPMENT

Chapter 1

Fly Rods

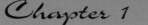

Parts of a fly rod include
the (1) Fighting butt, (2) Reel seat, (3) Grip, (4) Hookkeeper, (5) Butt section, (6) Stripping guide, (7) Ferrule (male), (8) Ferrule (female), (9) Tip section, (10) Snake guides, and (11) Tip-top.

Now that you have decided to start fly fishing, you must outfit yourself with an appropriate fly-fishing outfit. By outfit, I mean a fly rod, fly reel, and flyline. It is extremely important that your fly-fishing outfit is properly balanced, and will be suited for the type of fly fishing that you plan to do. The best place to get a good outfit is at a specialty fly-fishing store. The employees are often avid fly anglers and can provide a wealth of knowledge of how to put together the right outfit for you, as well as advice on many other aspects of fly fishing. Most metropolitan areas have at least one, if not several, such stores. If you don't live in an area with a fly shop, use the information in this chapter to help you choose an outfit yourself at a general sporting goods store or a mail order catalog, or in the Internet.

The last thing that you want to do is to try to learn to fly fish with an old, unbalanced outfit that once belonged to your dad or grandpa. Some old fly rods can be fun to fish with once in a while for nostalgia, but for learning purposes, the best old rod ever made can't compare to an inexpensive modern rod balanced with the right reel and line.

Let's start by selecting the right rod for you.

Weight Ratings

Fly rods are "rated" by what weight flyline they will cast. Simply put, the heavier the rod weight, the stiffer the rod must be to cast a thicker, heavier flyline. The heavier the flyline is, the larger the fly that can be cast. Remember that when you are fly casting, you aren't really casting the fly at all; you are casting the flyline, and the fly is being brought along for the ride. This is the opposite of spin fishing, where you are casting the lure, and the weight of the lure is pulling the line out.

Most prospective fly anglers have one or two favorite species they want to fish. For instance, you may want to fish for trout and sunfish, or maybe you're more interested in bigger game, such as bass and pike. Or you may be interested in fishing for all of these fish and more.

If you were spin fishing, a light rod that would be appropriate for smaller fish, such as sunfish and stream trout, wouldn't be a good choice for largemouth bass. Oh sure, you could go with a compromise 6-ft. medium-action spinning rod with 8-lb. test line spooled on the reel. An outfit like this can be made to work in a wide variety of fishing situations, but it wouldn't cast a tiny panfish jig very well. You also wouldn't stand much of a chance of pulling a big largemouth out of heavy cover with this outfit.

Just as in spin fishing, your fly-fishing outfit should be appropriate for the type of fish and the conditions.

See the chart for the appropriate fly rod for the fish you want to catch.

You can see that it is easy to pick one rod that will work for a variety of species, within reason. For example, a 5- or 6-weight would work great if sunfish, crappies, and trout were your quarry. Likewise, the pursuit of bass, pike, or steelhead would justify picking an 8- or even a 9-weight rod.

If you try to spread yourself too thin, like trying to make one rod work for pike, bass, trout, and sunfish, you will have to make some serious sacrifices. If you went with the ideal pike rod, a 9-weight, it would seem like a big ol' club when angling for sunfish. If you opted for the ideal sunfish rod, a 5-weight, you wouldn't come close to being able to cast a pike fly. So what is the answer?

After many years of working in fly shops myself, I have learned that many prospective fly anglers want the mythical, magical all-around fly rod that will work for all fly-fishing situations.

While it's true that a middle-of-the-road fly rod, like a 6- or 7-weight, could be made to work in many fly-fishing situations, it might not be ideal for any one type of fishing you want to do. The bottom line is that there is no magical all-around fly rod. Decide which

Matching Fly Rod Weight to Fish Type

Species	Rod Weight
Sunfish	4, 5, 6
Trout (in streams)	4, 5, 6
Crappies	4, 5, 6
Trout (in lakes)	5, 6, 7
Smallmouth Bass	6, 7, 8
Largemouth Bass	7, 8, 9
Steelhead	7, 8, 9
Salmon	8, 9, 10
Northern Pike	8, 9, 10

type of fish you want to go after most often, and choose your rod by referring to the chart.

For example, if you picked largemouth bass as your primary target, the ideal rod for you is an 8-weight.

Next, decide what other fish you might use your rod for. For instance, if you picked crappies as your second choice, a 6-weight would be the ideal rod to catch them. In this instance, a 7-weight would be a good compromise for both large-mouth bass and crappies.

Let's say that, instead, your second choice was trout in streams. A 5-weight would be the ideal rod to catch them. But trying to find a compromise rod for both largemouth bass and stream trout wouldn't be practical. A 6-weight might be too light for largemouth bass, and a 7-weight wouldn't have the finesse stream trout often require. In this instance, there isn't a good compromise rod. You will just have to remember

that largemouth bass were your first choice and your 8-weight rod will also work great for smallmouth bass, steelhead, pike, and salmon.

If you really want to fly fish for smaller fish, such as sunfish and trout, as well as larger predators, such as bass and pike, you might just have to accept that—just as in spin fishing—more that one rod is necessary. Remember that almost all experienced fly rod-ders have at least two, if not several, rods.

When it comes down to making the final decision about which weight your first rod will be, you will usually be deciding between two rod weights. My advice is to always pick the heavier one. First of all, I think that most people have an easier time learning how to cast with a heavier rod. Second, it's bet-ter to have a little more power to get the fly to its target. Too many beginning fly anglers—as well as experienced ones—make

the sport more difficult than it has to be by choosing a rod that is too light.

Some inexpensive rods will come rated for two line weights. It has been my experience that these rods almost always cast easier if you use the heavier line that is recommended.

Rod Length

Now that you have deter-mined which weight fly rod to get, there are a few other fac-tors to consider.

The first is which length rod to purchase. Most fly rods are much longer than your average spinning rod. A beginner might be put off by a 9-ft. rod, but this has almost become the standard length in the industry. Older fly-fishing manuals often recommended 7- or 8-ft. rods, but these writings usually date back to the days when fly rods

Graphite is the lightest material used to make mod-ern fly rods. Graphite rods are made from sheets of car-bon-fiber material wrapped around a tapered steel form, called a mandrel.

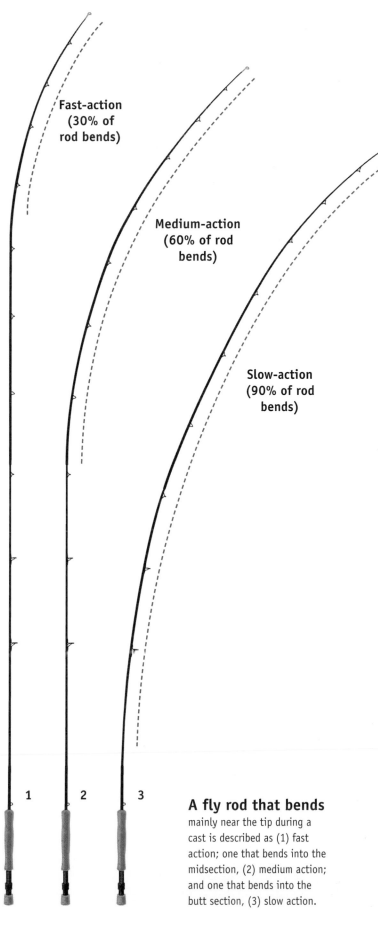

**Fast-action
(30% of
rod bends)**

**Medium-action
(60% of rod
bends)**

**Slow-action
(90% of rod
bends)**

1 2 3

A fly rod that bends
mainly near the tip during a
cast is described as (1) fast
action; one that bends into the
midsection, (2) medium action;
and one that bends into the
butt section, (3) slow action.

were made of fiberglass or
bamboo. A 9-ft. fly rod made of
fiberglass or bamboo feels
incredibly heavy in hand; therefore, back then shorter lengths
were often preferred. Now
that virtually all fly rods
are made of lightweight
graphite, rods 8 or 9 ft.
long are the way to go. A
long rod will make it easier to
cast, control, and pick up your
flyline. I do have a few longer
rods for big rivers, and a few
that are shorter for tiny creeks,
but if I had to pick one rod
length, it would be a 9-footer.

You may decide that a slightly longer or shorter rod will be
best for the fishing you will do
the most.

Rod Action

The next decision is to
choose the appropriate "action"
or "taper" of your rod.

Actions in fly rods range from
slow to very fast, but most fall
into the medium to medium-
fast category. A rod with a slow
action bends almost evenly
from the tip of the rod to the
grip. A rod with a fast action
bends mainly in the upper third
of the rod only.

It has often been said that
beginners learn how to cast
best on slow- to medium-action
rods. It has been my experience,
however, that medium-fast- to
fast-action rods are the easiest
to learn on.

Most fly shops will allow you
to take a rod out on the lawn for
a few test casts. You can probably even get a staff member to
give you some valuable casting
pointers in the process.

Cost

How much should you expect to pay for a fly rod? I have looked at and cast modern fly rods that range in price from under $50 to over $600. It should come as no surprise that in fly rods, like everything else in this world, you get what you pay for.

I have had many beginners show up at a fly-casting class with a cheap rod that was purchased at a "mega-mart" store. On several occasions, I couldn't even make these rods work. Beginners justify buying a cheap rod by saying that they're a beginner, they don't know if they're going to like it, they don't know how much they'll get to fish with it, and so on.

Buying a cheap rod will always compromise your ability to learn how to cast. While I would never expect a beginner to drop $600 on his or her first rod, you do need to have a rod with a basic level of quality if you want to become a proficient caster.

I got my first fly rod when I was eight years old. It was a pretty cheap fiberglass model that came from Herter's (now defunct). The flex of that rod was just awful by today's standards, but I somehow managed to catch many trout and panfish on it. It wasn't until I was a teenager that my grandpa gave me a good fly rod, a little 3-weight. I couldn't believe how much lighter it was!

As soon as I had this rod in my possession, my already high level of interest in fly fishing increased tenfold. I used it whenever possible, including situations where it was really too light to be practical. I have been slowly accumulating good fly rods ever since, making sure that I always have a rod that is appropriate for the fishing that I'm doing.

Levels of fly rods

Most fly rods fall into one of three levels of quality, price, and performance:

• Good enough to get you by. Rods in this category will work great when matched with an appropriate flyline, and make it easy for anyone to be able to afford a functional fly rod. Rods in this category usually cost between $75 and $150. Some good examples of these rods are Redington's Redfly and RS2, and St. Croix's Pro Graphite and Imperial rods.

• As good as you really need. Rods in this category are usually made with better materials and have better tapers that will allow a higher level of performance to suit almost anyone's needs. Rods in this category usually cost between $200 and $350. Some examples of rods in this category are Sage's DS2, Diamondback's VSR, and G. Loomis' GL3.

• As good as it gets. Rods in this category are the pride of the fly-fishing industry. They have been carefully designed by experts to be the lightest, fastest, most accurate casting machines possible. And they keep getting better (and more expensive) every year. If it is within your means, you will not be disappointed with one of these rods. Rods in this category range in price from $400 to over $600. Some examples of rods in this category are Redington's DFR, Sage's XP, and G. Loomis' GLX.

The specific rods that I mentioned are all great choices.

However, there are many other models of rods out there that are as good or maybe even better. Be sure to get a rod made by a well-known fly rod manufacturer and when in doubt, rely on recommendations from your local fly shop.

Things to Remember When Buying Your First Fly Rod.

• If possible, buy from a reputable fly shop.

• Get a rod made by a well-known fly rod manufacturer.

• Purchase the best one you can afford.

• Don't get a rod that is too short or too light.

• "Fast" rods are typically easier to cast than "slow" rods.

Chapter 2

Reels, Lines & Leaders

After you have selected the right fly rod, your flyfishing outfit won't be complete until you have the right reel, line, and leader setup.

Reels

Fly fishermen around the world constantly debate the importance of having a quality fly reel. It's just a line holder! is often said by proponents of going the cheap route. It's true, a fly reel is a very simple piece of equipment when compared with a spinning or baitcasting reel, and in many cases, you bring the fish in by stripping in the line through your rod hand, not using the reel at all.

In many light-duty fly-fishing situations, the reel that's on your rod is of little consequence, as long as it is the proper size.

But don't use the line holder statement alone as an excuse to get the cheapest reel there is. A quality reel with a good "disc" drag is a joy to fish with and will last for many years, while a cheap reel with a "clicker drag" will probably burn out within a few years of heavy use.

You will never realize how valuable a smooth reel with a disc drag is until you have a big fish on that really takes out some line. Now your fly reel has suddenly become more than just a line holder! If you start out with a quality disc-drag reel, you will never wish you had bought a clicker reel instead. Just as with fly rods, you get what you pay for in fly reels.

Since the selection of the fly reel is probably more of a personal decision than any other piece of your fly-fishing equipment, I will discuss the features of several popular reels that range in price from under $50 to over $300. You can decide which reel will be appropriate for the fishing you will be doing and your budget. Of course, there are many other models available that are just as good, but these reels are ones that I am familiar with and that have proven themselves—and virtually all fly reels are based on one of these designs.

If your local fly shop staffer recommends another reel, take the advice if the reel has the features you're looking for and it fits your budget.

Here are six models I recommend:

Cortland Vista Click

This is a popular choice with beginners. Its simple construction and low price (about $30) are its main selling points. The drag on this reel is provided by a spring-loaded plastic or metal pawl situated on the inside of the frame that clicks against teeth on the inside of the spool.

This arrangement has proven to be reliable, especially when fishing for fish that don't take out any line, such as panfish or small trout. It also features an exposed rim on its spool that allows you to apply additional pressure when stripping off line, or when you hook a fish that makes a run long enough to pull line off the reel.

The reel is constructed of cast (or molded) aluminum. Notice that there are two pawls (see page 16). Left- or right-hand retrieve is determined by which of these pawls is standing up. You can increase the tension somewhat by standing both pawls up, but you can never really have true stopping power.

Be aware that clicker- or ratchet-pawl reels can backlash if you strip line off too hard, or if a fish makes a sudden, fast run. Because of the design all these reels sound loud, and there is no changing it.

Cortland's Vista disc-drag

This is one of the least expensive disc-drag reels available. If you're looking for a reel that has some real braking power without costing too much, this one's a good choice.

The reel is constructed of cast aluminum, which makes it a bit heavy and not as smooth as some more expensive models, but it's still a good value at around $60.

The drag works like this: When you tighten the drag knob on the back of the reel, it puts pressure on the small gear, which in turn puts pressure on the center disc. Around the inside of this disc, there is a series of "ramps" that go all the way around the disc. The ramps are sloped on one side and vertical on the other. On the inside of the spool is a spring-loaded pin. This pin rides over the sloped side of the ramps when you reel in, but catches on the vertical side when line is pulled out.

The reel can be switched from right- to left-hand retrieve by flipping over the center disc.

Vista reels are noisier than other disc-drag reels, but the outgoing click can be eliminated by removing the clicker spring. This will not affect the performance of the drag in any way.

Scientific Anglers System 2 series

For two decades this design has proven to be a winner. It is a disc-drag reel that utilizes the caliper style of braking, similar to that used in cars.

When you tighten the drag knob on the back of the reel it puts pressure on the drag pads that grip the disc. In the center

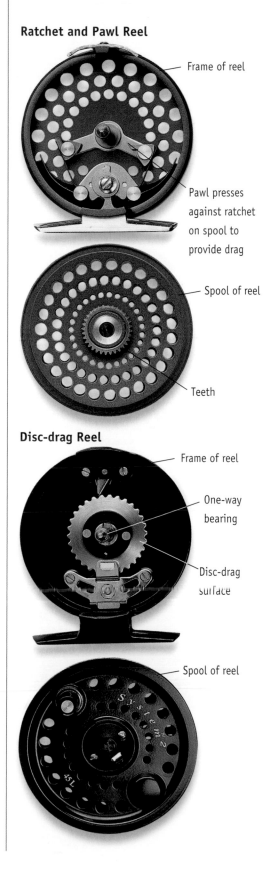

Reel Drag Systems

Ratchet and Pawl Reel

Frame of reel

Pawl presses against ratchet on spool to provide drag

Spool of reel

Teeth

Disc-drag Reel

Frame of reel

One-way bearing

Disc-drag surface

Spool of reel

Cortland Vista Click

Cortland's Vista disc-drag

Scientific Anglers System 2 series

Redington RS2

Ross Reels Gunnison series

Abel Super 8

of the disc is a one-way bearing that is engaged by two pegs on the inside of the spool. When you reel in, the bearing spins freely. When line is pulled out, the bearing won't turn and the drag is engaged.

System 2 reels are manufactured by first being cast, and then machined down to the right tolerances.

To change from right- to left-hand retrieve, flip over the center disc.

Depending on which size you need, System 2 reels sell for between $120 and $150.

Redington RS2

In recent years there has been considerable hype surrounding large arbor fly reels. As the name implies, the spools on reels of this design have a much larger spool than standard reels, with an open center. If properly designed, they are also somewhat wider than standard reels.

Large arbor reels are not new; I have noticed reels of this design in antique tackle books that date back to the 1800s. Their benefits include faster line retrieval, better line storage (larger coils), and a consistent drag with any amount of line out. While these benefits are minimal in most freshwater situations, they are still worth checking out.

One of the best of the new large arbor reels is Redington's RS2. The drag surface on this machined aluminum reel is a synthetic fiber washer between two stainless steel washers. Tightening the drag knob on the back of the reel increases the force put on the drag.

Inside the spool is a one-way roller bearing. When you reel in, the rollers spin freely on the spindle above the drag washers. When line is pulled out, the rollers grab the spindle and engage the drag.

RS2 reels range in price from $130 to $150, depending on the size.

Ross Reels Gunnison series

This company is well known for producing high-quality machined fly reels at moderate prices. Reels that are "machined" are actually carved out of blocks of solid, high-quality aluminum. Ross' Gunnison series of reels is perhaps their best known.

One thing you'll notice right away on a machined reel like this one is that the walls of the frame and spool are thinner than on cast reels. Reel parts that are machined are much stronger than cast parts, so the manufacturer is able to make all the parts thinner, making the reel weigh less.

Another advantage of machined reels is that the spool and frame fit together precisely, making for smooth performance.

The drag on the Gunnison reel works like this: When you tighten the drag knob on the back of the frame, it pulls the disc, made of a space-age plastic called delrin, against the frame on the reel. The drag is actually from the friction between these two surfaces. Notice that the disc has sloped ramps on it similar to the Cortland Vista.

The large cylinder coming out of the center of the disc contains sealed ball bearings that the spool rides on, adding to the smoothness of the reel. Inside the spool are two spring-loaded pins that ride

over the ramps when you reel in, and catch on the vertical side of the ramps when line is pulled out. The anodized finish protects the reel from scratches and corrosion.

Gunnison reels sell for around $200 to $250, more expensive than most, but a good value for anglers wanting their fly reel to be more than a line holder.

Abel Big Game series

No matter what consumer product you're shopping for, you can always spend more than you could imagine if you demand the very best. A serious golfer wouldn't think twice about spending several hundred dollars on a driver; and to an avid upland game hunter, spending $1,000 wouldn't be out of the question for a great double-barreled shotgun. If you really appreciate fine-quality workmanship, consider getting a premium-quality fly reel. There are several manufacturers that make reels of this caliber, and Abel is among the best of them.

The design of the Big Game series of reels is actually quite simple. All the parts of these reels are machined with an anodized finish. The drag surface is cork, which has been proven to offer the most reliable and smoothest drag possible.

When reeling in, the spool is pressed against the disc, and the two turn together. The teeth on the outside of the disc click against the spring-loaded pawl located inside the frame. When line is pulled out, the teeth catch on the pawl, and the spool turns under tension against the cork drag surface.

This tension is regulated by how tightly you turn the drag knob located on the back of the frame. The more you turn the drag knob, the more pressure is put on the spool against the cork.

At around $400, these reels may be beyond what most people can justify spending for a fly reel, but they will give you—as well as your children and grandchildren—a lifetime of use.

Things to Remember When Choosing a Reel

- Be sure the reel is the proper size for the rod. It should hold the flyline plus at least 100 yards of backing.

- If all your fly fishing will be for bass or panfish, a clicker reel is adequate.

- Disc-drag reels are quieter and smoother than clicker reels.

- If you plan to fish for steelhead or salmon, a disc drag is mandatory to slow down the fast runs these fish often make.

- Machined reels are usually lighter in weight than cast reels.

- Quality reels will last a lifetime.

Flylines

I don't think that any fly-fishing expert would question the importance of having a quality floating flyline. At first glance, a flyline looks like a plastic-coated piece of string, and basically that's what it is. However, a quality flyline is actually tapered throughout much of its length, and the way it is tapered is just one of many variables that affect how it will cast. There are several different tapers available, including many subtle variations.

The three basic types are level, double-taper, and weight-forward (the latter also having sinking varieties).

Level

This flyline is the least expensive line you can buy, and the last one you want. Level flylines won't be found in any fly shops because they really lack the performance that someone who is serious about the sport requires. They will load your rod okay, but offer no delicacy in presentation, and minimal distance casting opportunities.

Level line has no taper.

Double-taper

This type of line has been popular for many years. Proponents of these lines claim better delicacy in presentation, and you can turn the line around when the end

Double-taper line has a taper at the front and the back of the line.

you've been using wears out, getting another couple of seasons out of your investment. If all of your fishing will be on small streams where casting beyond 30 ft. isn't a factor, double-taper lines will work just fine.

Weight-forward

For most situations, a weight-forward line is the best choice. This type of line does a great job of loading the rod with a minimal amount of line out for short casts, as well as being able to easily cast longer distances.

Weight-forward line has its thickest portion in the front 1/3 part of the line.

While there are many variations on this design, the basic principle still applies: The line is much thicker in the front third. This thickest portion of the line is called the "belly." It tapers in the front to offer some delicacy in presentation, and also tapers in the rear to form the much-thinner running line.

All of the flyline manufacturers offer weight-forward taper lines in many configurations. Some variations have a longer, thinner front taper for more delicate presentations. These lines actually allow for more delicacy than any double-taper line.

One popular design is the "bass bug" taper. These lines have a very short front taper and a short but thick belly and are designed to cast large bass or pike flies. For most situations, though, a general-purpose weight-forward line is what you want.

Line weight is measured in grains and determines what size fly you can comfortably cast. The 3-part code (WF-5-F) on the packaging helps you identify the line shape, as well as its weight and whether it floats or sinks.

Sinking

Sinking lines vary as to how much of the line is weighted to sink. Here, the darker portion represents the sink-tip.

There are many different types of sinking line available. While it is usually most enjoyable to catch fish on or near the surface, sometimes you just have to get down deep. You can purchase spare spools for most fly reels. Having a spare spool with a sinking line on it enables you to go deep when conditions call for it. Depending on which sinking line you get, it is possible to get a fly down as deep as about 15 ft.

Here are a few of the most common sinking lines and their general applications:

• Intermediate lines sink at an extremely slow rate (about 1 in. per second). They work great for using sub-surface flies on lakes, especially in windy conditions. Since an intermediate line is denser than a floating line, it really cuts through the wind, and sinks just below the waves.

• Full-sinking lines come in many different sink rates, up to 8 in. per second. These lines work best in lakes when you're trying to get down deep near drop-offs or deep weedlines.

• Sink-tip lines are floating lines with a 5-ft. to 15-ft. sinking tip. These lines work great for deep fishing in rivers since the floating rear portion will still allow you to control, or mend, the line after it has been cast. They also come in many different sink rates from 1 in. to 5 in. per second.

• Integrated-head lines are a more modern version of the old sinking shooting heads, which are used when you're trying to cast long distances and get deep fast. An integrated-head line has a front sinking portion, or head, that is rated in grains instead of line weight. The head is usually between 20 ft. and 30 ft. long. It is followed by a thin running line that can be either floating or intermediate.

Things to Remember when Picking a Flyline

• Buy the best flyline you can afford.

• A weight-forward line is the best all-around line.

• It is usually best to buy a line that is the size your rod is rated for.

• If your rod is rated for two line sizes, buy the heavier line.

• A floating line is what you will be using the most, and what you should learn on, but one or more sinking lines can be useful.

Leaders & Tippets

People who are new to fly fishing are often amazed at how thick and heavy a flyline appears. Because of that thickness, you don't tie your fly directly to the flyline. Instead, you attach a tapered leader to the end of the flyline, and attach your fly to the end of the leader, called a tippet.

Tapered leader

Tapered leaders are usually made of nylon monofilament, as are other types of fishing line. They are usually between 6 ft. and 10 ft. long, and come in many different configurations and strengths.

The butt end of a tapered leader is quite thick, usually measuring about 0.022 in. to 0.024 in. in diameter. This is equal to about 30-lb. to 40-lb. monofilament line. This thickness usually matches the diameter (and stiffness) of the tip of your flyline. The leader usually stays this thick for about the first third, and then gradually tapers, without knots, to form the tippet, which is the last, lightest part of the tapered leader.

If it weren't for knotless, tapered leaders, we'd have to taper them ourselves by knotting many pieces of different-diameter mono lines together to form a tapered leader. Some anglers believe that a hand-knotted leader actually works better. I don't doubt that hand-knotted leaders work just fine—go ahead and make some if you like—but I'd rather spend my non-fishing time tying flies or practicing casting than tying pieces of mono together.

You can usually make a tapered leader last for at least a couple of outings, barring any serious casting disasters. You will need to add more tippet when the provided tippet (usually the last 20 in. to 30 in.) becomes too short or non-existent from inevitable fly changes. This is accomplished by tying a very simple knot, the double-surgeon's knot. (See Chapter 3 for instructions to tie this and other common knots.)

Tippets can usually be replaced three or four times without affecting the overall performance of the leader. Tippet material is usually sold in 30-yd. spools, and a spool usually sells for around $3.50. It is a good idea to use tippet material from the same manufacturer that made the leaders you use. Sometimes there are subtle variations in the formulas used by the different manufacturers that can cause problems in knot strength if you mix and match brands.

As a rule of thumb, your leader should be about the same length as your rod, at least when using a floating line. Sinking lines require the use of short, 3–6ft. leaders. How strong the tippet should be is determined by a few factors like the size of fish likely to be encountered, the size of the fly being used, and how wary the fish are due to water clarity.

The shorter and heavier the leader is, the easier it is to cast, especially on short casts or with large flies, but the less delicate it will be. Likewise, a long, light leader will give you a very delicate presentation, but it won't "turn over" well with large flies or in windy conditions. Don't make life difficult for yourself by using a long light leader when you don't need to. The accompanying chart will give you a guideline for proper leader lengths and strengths under different conditions.

Tippet

The strength of the tippet is usually between 2- and 12-lb. test. (The "test" is a measurement of the breaking strength of the tippet.) You might think that you can get around buying tapered leaders by simply tying 6 or 8 ft. of the desired pound test line to the end of your flyline. Try this, and you'll soon realize the importance of the tapered leader.

When your flyline unrolls at the end of a cast, it carries a certain amount of energy with it. This energy must travel down the leader to the fly in order to get your cast to lay out nice and straight. If instead of a tapered leader, you tried to use

Leader Lengths & Strengths

Species	Length	Lb.-test Weight	X Size
Panfish	7¹/₂ ft.	4–8 lbs.	5x–3x
Trout	7¹/₂–12 ft.	2–8 lbs.	7x–3x
Bass	6–9 ft.	8–15 lbs.	3x–0x
Pike	4–6 ft.	20 lbs.	N/A
Steelhead	4–9 ft.	6–10 lbs.	4x–2x

8 ft. of 6-lb.-test, the energy of the cast wouldn't be able to transfer from the thick flyline directly through the leader to the fly, and your cast would land in a heap. With a tapered leader, the energy of the cast travels down the line, and flows down the leader to the tippet, and your fly lands perfectly.

Before proceeding any further, let's talk about how you know what size tippet is right for you. Tippet sizes are often expressed by using an x-number. The larger the number is, the finer the tippet. So, 5x is thinner than 4x, which is thinner than 3x, and so on. Heavy (or thick) tippet sizes, like 0x or 1x, are typically used for fishing large flies for bass or very large trout. Finer tippet sizes like 6x or 7x are reserved for times when spooky stream trout are taking very small flies.

It is important to keep in mind that the x-number reflects the diameter of the tippet, not the pound-test rating. If you check the pound-test rating of 3x tippet material from several different manufacturers, you'll notice that it will range from 6 lbs. to 9 lbs., but the diameter will always be 0.008 in.

In fly fishing, the diameter of your tippet is more important than the actual pound-test rating. It's always a compromise to determine the proper tippet size. A thinner tippet sometimes enables you to get more strikes, but a thicker tippet has a higher breaking strength and "turns over" better with a large fly.

Other advantages of using the heaviest tippet possible are that you won't have to retie your fly as often, and you'll be more likely to pull your fly free from snags.

As long as you are using a tippet size that is reasonable for the conditions, the actual pound test of the tippet is of little consequence. You really can't generate enough force with a fly rod to break even relatively light tippets, as long as all of the connections are secure.

Fluorocarbon

Fluorocarbon is a new tippet material that has become quite popular with some fly anglers. It is made from polyvinylidene fluouride, which has a few advantages over nylon. One is its low visibility underwater—in clear water, this can't be a bad thing.

Fluorocarbon is also extremely abrasion resistant, a plus when fishing in very snaggy water. It is also more dense than nylon, so it sinks faster.

I can only think of two negatives about fluorocarbon. First, it doesn't knot as smoothly as nylon unless the knot is well lubricated. Second, it is quite a bit more expensive than nylon, with a spool usually selling for $10 to $14.

Whether or not using fluorocarbon will actually get you more strikes is still up for debate. I know that I always have a couple of spools of it in my vest for tough conditions.

Things to Remember When Choosing Leaders & Tippets

• Always use a tapered leader.

• When using a floating line, the length of your leader, including the tippet, should be about the same length as your rod.

• When using sinking lines, keep your leader short—3 to 6 ft.

• Use tippets from the same manufacturer as your leaders.

• Tippets should be fresh; don't use any over 2 years old.

• Try fluorocarbon when ultra-clear water makes for tough conditions.

Tippet Ratings and Fly Sizes

X-rating	Diameter	Breaking-strength Rating	Fly Size Range
8x	.003 in.	1.0 – 1.8 lbs.	28 – 20
7x	.004 in.	1.1 – 2.5 lbs.	26 – 18
6x	.005 in.	1.4 – 3.5 lbs.	22 – 14
5x	.006 in.	2.4 – 4.8 lbs.	18 – 10
4x	.007 in.	3.1 – 6.0 lbs.	16 – 8
3x	.008 in.	3.8 – 8.5 lbs.	14 – 6
2x	.009 in.	4.5 – 11.5 lbs.	10 – 4

This chart shows the typical pound-test rating range for various-size tippets, and the fly hook sizes that typically work best for them. This chart is a guideline only, and specific circumstances may require you to vary from these recommendations.

Chapter 3

Knots

Placement of Knots

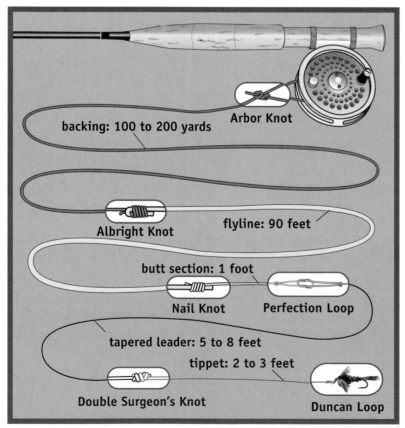

backing: 100 to 200 yards

Arbor Knot

Albright Knot

flyline: 90 feet

butt section: 1 foot

Nail Knot

Perfection Loop

tapered leader: 5 to 8 feet

tippet: 2 to 3 feet

Double Surgeon's Knot

Duncan Loop

The diagram above shows the proper sequence of knots for connecting the backing, flyline, butt section, leader, tippet and fly. These knots retain a high percentage of line strength when tied correctly.

If you purchase your fly-fishing outfit at a good fly shop, the staff members will be happy to assemble it for you by first winding on the proper amount of backing, securely attaching the backing to the flyline, and modifying the tip of the flyline to make leader changes easy.

If you purchased your outfit somewhere other than a fly shop, you're on your own to put it together. It really isn't that hard, and with my guidelines, you should have no problem.

Many people have the misconception that there are lots of tricky knots to be learned if you want to fly fish. In this chapter, I will describe several knots. None of them are all that difficult to learn, and if you practice tying them at home, re-rigging on the water should be no problem.

Outfit Assembly

First, decide if you want to reel with your right or left hand. If you cast with your right hand, set up your reel to crank in line with your left hand. By setting up like this you won't have to change the rod from your right to your left hand to reel in, and vice versa for lefties. Most reels come with the drag set to work when reeling with the left hand. If yours doesn't come this way, or if you want to reel in with your right hand, the reel should be converted before you proceed. The reel should come with instructions for doing this.

Backing to reel arbor

Attach the backing to the arbor of the reel. This is accomplished with an arbor knot, which is a very simple knot to tie.

It is important to have the proper amount of backing on your reel before attaching the flyline. Backing does several things for you. It fills up the spool to increase your retrieve rate. It also prevents your flyline from being stored in tiny coils against the arbor of the reel. Finally, if you should hook a fish that pulls off your entire flyline, you could fight the fish with the backing.

Backing is available as 20 or 30 lb., and is usually available in 100- or 250-yd. spools. It comes in several colors, and I like my backing to be a different color than the flyline. Your reel should come with a chart showing the recommended amount of backing it will hold with different-weight flylines.

Begin reeling the backing onto the reel. This will be much easier if you put the reel on the rod and run the backing through the guide closest to the reel first. If you can, have someone hold the spool of backing by sticking a pencil through the center of the spool and holding moderate tension on it while you reel in.

Trying to determine when you have exactly the right amount of backing on is a bit tricky. As a general rule, if the flyline you intend to put on the reel is an appropriate size for the reel, you should fill it about two-thirds to three-quarters full with backing before attaching the flyline. You can also try to visualize how much space the flyline takes up on the spool it comes on, and how it will fill up the space left on your reel.

Backing to flyline

Next, attach the backing to the flyline. On weight-forward lines, it is absolutely critical that you attach the backing to the proper end of the flyline. Fortunately, weight-forward lines

Arbor Knot

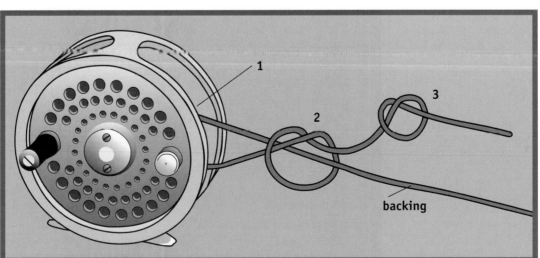

Use an arbor knot to attach backing. (1) Wrap backing around spool, then tie two overhand knots as shown. Tighten both knots. Pull on standing line until the first knot (2) tightens securely against the arbor. Keep pulling until the second knot (3) snugs up against the first knot (2).

come with this end marked with a tag that says "This end to reel." If, for some reason, your line isn't marked this way, run the whole line out off the spool to determine which end is the thicker, weight-forward end, and attach the backing to the thin, running line end.

If you decided to go with a double-taper line, it doesn't matter which end you attach to the backing.

The best knot for making this connection is the Albright knot. It looks harder to tie than it is, and you should be able to do it on your first or second try.

Flyline to reel

Now wind the flyline onto your reel. Again, have someone hold the spool of flyline for you by sticking a pencil through the center of the spool. For some reason, all of the flyline manufacturers package their lines on two-piece spools which can fall apart while you wind the line, creating a huge tangle. If this happens, it can mean several minutes of untangling the line, so make sure that the two sides of the spool stay together while you wind the line onto the reel. If you run out of room as you get to the tip of the flyline, strip the flyline back off and then remove some backing. It's okay if you don't quite fill the reel. It's always better to be a little light on backing than to be too heavy.

Leader to flyline

To attach a tapered leader to the flyline, you have a couple options. Many anglers tie the leader directly to the flyline with a nail knot (some people call it a tube knot). A properly tied nail knot is quite secure

Albright Knot

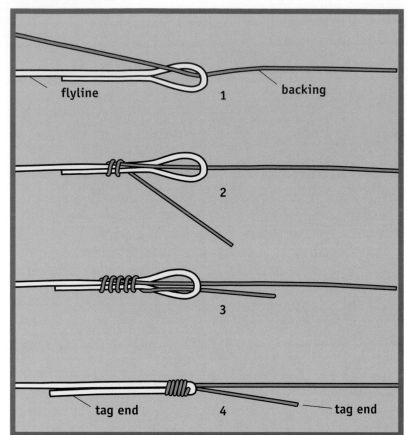

Attach backing to flyline with an Albright knot. (1) Double up last 2 inches of flyline and pass tag end of backing through loop. (2) Wind backing over itself and flyline at least five times. (3) Pass backing through loop as shown. (4) Tighten slowly; trim ends closely.

and will go through the guides easily. This is the one knot that gives novice fly fishermen around the world fits.

Don't expect your first attempts to turn out perfect. If you can get your hands on an old flyline and some heavy (0.022 in. to 0.026 in.) mono, you should practice tying this knot. Your nail knot doesn't have to look as perfect as the one shown here, but it should be fairly smooth, and stand up to a vigorous pull test.

When you tie a leader to your flyline with this knot, try to keep the tag end of the flyline less than 1/2 in. long. If each time you tied this knot you

ended up with a 3-in. tag end, you would soon use up the whole tip section of your flyline and be into the front taper. This would drastically affect how the line casts. Always trim the tag ends as close as you can so the knot will flow easily through the guides.

To avoid having to tie a new nail knot each time you change leaders, you can attach a 12-in. butt section of heavy (0.022-in. to 0.026-in.) mono to the flyline with a nail knot and put a loop knot in the end of it. By then putting a loop knot in the butt end of the leader, you can attach leaders with a loop-to-loop connection. A perfection loop is the

Nail Knot

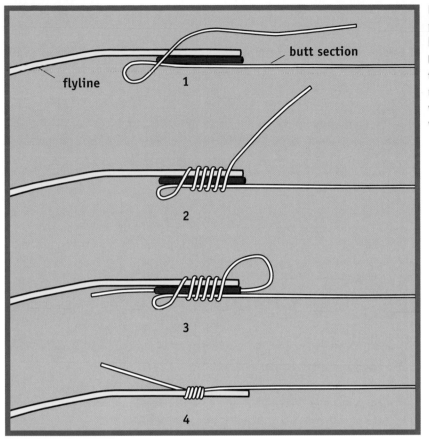

flyline

butt section

1

2

3

4

Use a nail knot to attach mono butt section to fly-line. (1) Place tube alongside fly-line, and loop butt section alongside tube. Follow steps (2) and (3), then remove tube. (4) Tighten knot slowly while using your fingernails to position wraps. Closely trim tags.

Tie a perfection loop at end of mono butt section. (1) Begin with 6-in. tag and form loop A as shown. (2) Form a second loop B, hold in place, then cross tag on top of loop B. (3) Hold tag in place and pass loop B through loop A. (4) Pull loop B until tight; trim.

Tie perfection loops on all tapered leaders (inset). That way, you can use a loop-to-loop connection to quickly change leaders as needed. (1) Pass loop of leader over that of butt section. (2) Thread other end of leader through loop of butt section. (3) Pull both sections to tighten.

Perfection Loop

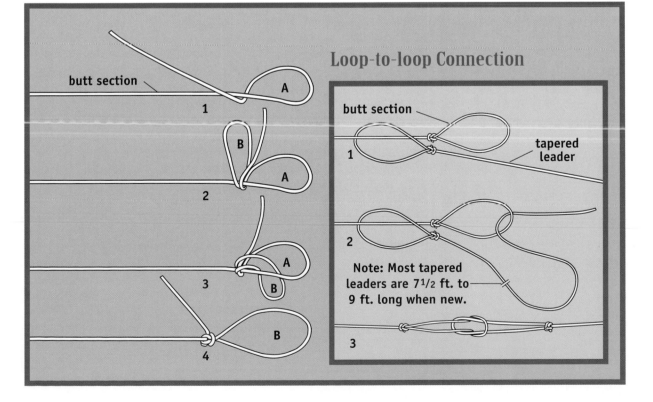

butt section

1

B

A

2

A

3

A

B

4

B

Loop-to-loop Connection

butt section

1

tapered leader

2

Note: Most tapered leaders are 7¹/2 ft. to 9 ft. long when new.

3

preferred knot for making this loop. With practice, this knot can be tied in seconds, and you can make the loop smaller than would be possible with other loop knots.

If you don't have any heavy mono available, attach your first leader with a nail knot as instructed. When you want to change leaders, cut off the old leader, leaving about 18 in. and tie a loop knot in what's left. This is now your butt section.

If you are unable to tie a nail knot, another great way to attach leaders to your flyline is by using a braided-loop connection. While I don't trust these knots as much as I do a good nail knot, they are very popular, and many anglers have used them for years with no problems.

To attach a braided-loop connection (but don't try this on the water), gradually work the end of the flyline into the open end of the loop and "inchworm" it all the way in. These loops come packaged with shrink tubing to help hold the loop in place. To get the tubing in place, you must push the end of the loop through the tubing (about 1/2 in. long). Slide the tubing up so it overlaps the frayed end of the braided loop.

Now shrink the tubing using a hot light bulb or iron. A drop of Super Glue where the tip of the flyline fits inside the braided loop gives a little added insurance against the braided loop pulling off the end of your flyline.

Tippet to fly

As mentioned earlier, your tapered leader has a tippet built into it, usually the front 2 ft. You can tie your fly right onto it. If you want to add more tippet to your leader, this is easily done with a double surgeon's knot. Almost any experienced fly angler knows this one and can demonstrate tying it. This is a knot that you will use every time out, so make sure to practice it.

There are dozens of knots used to tie on a fly, and all fly fishermen have their favorite. I've tried most of them and none are as easy to tie or as consistently strong as the Duncan loop, or the plain old "clinch" knot. These knots snug down well, particularly with heavy or fluorocarbon tippet, if you lubricate it with saliva just before you tighten it.

There are a few other knots that can be useful in certain fly-fishing situations, but these are the basic ones you need to get started.

Making a Braided Loop Connnection (Option for Attaching Leader to Flyline)

Squeeze the end of the connector to open braids; insert end of flyline.

Finished connector

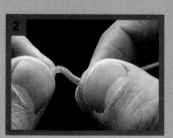

Work end of flyline into connector by alternately squeezing the braids and pushing on the line. Continue until line is as far into connector as possible; it must be in at least 2 in. to be secure.

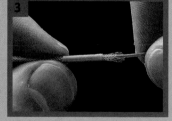

Slide plastic sleeve that comes with connector down to cover the braided end, which may be frayed.

Dab Super Glue® on the connector, if desired. Because the connector operates on the "Chinese finger trap" principle, however, this step is usually unnecessary.

Double Surgeon's Knot

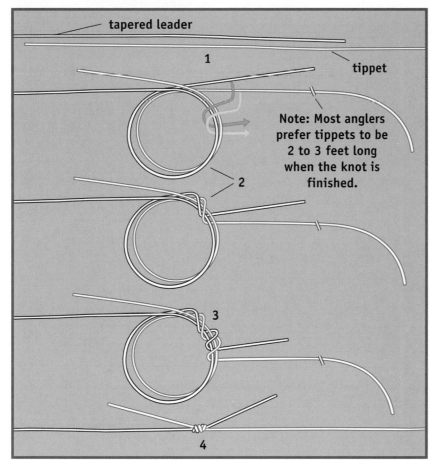

tapered leader

1

tippet

Note: Most anglers prefer tippets to be 2 to 3 feet long when the knot is finished.

2

3

4

The double surgeon's knot is used for attaching tippet to leader.

(1) Place tippet next to leader, then (2) form an overhand knot. (3) Form a double overhand knot by passing same ends through loop a second time. (4) Tighten by pulling all four ends slowly; trim tags.

Duncan Loop

A Duncan loop can be snugged up with loop open to allow fly to swing freely on tippet (shown here), or pulled tight against hook. The loop may close from the pull of a fish, but you can easily reopen it by carefully sliding knot back. Closely trim tag.

tippet

1   2   3   4

Chapter 4

Flies

Stonefly Adult
(5 times actual size)

Black Stimulator
(mimics stonefly adult)

Of all of the different aspects of fly fishing, the flies themselves get more press than anything else pertaining to the sport. This is because flies are interesting, colorful and artistic, and they have character. All fly tiers have their own style that gives their flies a unique look. A fellow fly angler will often ask for a peek into one of my fly boxes, but no one has ever asked to look in my leader wallet or to peruse my split shot selection. These items, while important, are very boring to look at when compared to flies!

The first flies ever made were tied to imitate insects. Imitating insects is the cornerstone of fly fishing, and is what usually comes to mind to most people when you mention fly fishing.

While some fish do feed on bugs, some are more likely to feed on other fish, crustaceans, leeches, or other larger food items. There are also flies that imitate these other food items.

Entomology

Before going into any more specifics on flies, you're going to need a crash course in entomology. Despite what other books or magazine articles may lead you to believe, you don't need to memorize the life cycle of every aquatic insect found in the area that you fish, but a good working knowledge of mayflies, caddisflies, stoneflies, and midges is mandatory if you plan to be successful, especially with stream trout. For other types of fish, entomology is of less importance, but can still be valuable in certain situations.

Mayflies

The most recognized and possibly the most important type of aquatic insect for fly anglers, is the mayfly. Different species hatch at somewhat predictable times in a given region each year, and hatch charts show the approximate times of their emergence. Different species of mayflies often are referred to by their common names, such as sulphurs, Hendricksons, March browns, rather than their Latin names.

Mayflies live most of their lives as an immature form called nymphs, spending their days underwater. Some nymphs live in silt, some live in weeds, and some cling to rocks and logs. For stream trout fishermen, the rock-clinging nymphs are the most important. To really get a feel for what these nymphs look like, the next time you are at a trout stream, pull up some midstream rocks and logs and look at what's on them. Knowing exactly what species any bug is isn't really necessary. By look-ing at the nymphs found in the streams you fish, you will be able to determine the size, shape, and color of the nymphs that are typical to your home waters. This will enable you to fill your fly box with imitations that are appropriate.

After a mayfly nymph has matured (usually in 1 to 2 years) most species swim to the surface to become adults. They often have to struggle in the surface film to break out of their nymphal shuck before they can complete their metamorphosis. In this stage the mayfly is referred to as an emerger. It usually takes only a couple of seconds for this metamorphosis to be completed, but sometimes it can take much longer. A fly fished in the surface film can be very successful when fish are feeding on emergers.

Once the mayfly has discarded its nymphal shuck, it floats

Mayfly Life Cycle

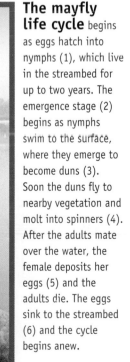

The mayfly life cycle begins as eggs hatch into nymphs (1), which live in the streambed for up to two years. The emergence stage (2) begins as nymphs swim to the surface, where they emerge to become duns (3). Soon the duns fly to nearby vegetation and molt into spinners (4). After the adults mate over the water, the female deposits her eggs (5) and the adults die. The eggs sink to the streambed (6) and the cycle begins anew.

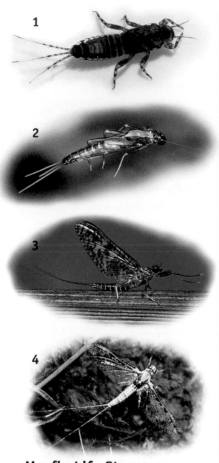

Mayfly Life Stages: (1) nymph, (2) emerger, (3) dun, (4) spinner.

Caddisfly Life Stages: (1) larvae, (2) pupa, (3) adult.

on the surface waiting for its sailboat-like wings to dry. Usually this takes only a few seconds. On rainy or humid days, it can take several minutes. At this stage of life, mayflies are known as duns, and are very vulnerable to fish. A good hatch of duns is what most fly anglers dream about. When there is an abundance of duns on the surface, most fish won't pass up this buffet of bugs flowing over their heads.

Once a mayfly's wings have dried, it flies to nearby streamside shrubbery and finds a mate. After mating, the females return to the water to lay their eggs. At this stage of their life they are called spinners. Their once-proud, upright wings now lie spent at their sides as they die after laying their eggs. With some species of mayflies, this is the most important stage to fly fishermen. When encountering a "spinner fall," an angler would be wise to have an assortment of spent-wing patterns.

Caddisflies

For anglers targeting trout or other insect-eating fish, the second most important aquatic insect is the caddisfly. As an adult, these insects resemble moths flying over the surface of the water. As nymphs (technically called larva), they are found on the stream bottom living in caddis cases made of bits of sand, wood, or gravel. These cases are reminiscent of cocoons made by moths and butterflies.

A rock or log pulled out of a stream with a good population of caddisflies will be covered with caddis cases. Fish will eagerly feed on these cased

Match the Hatch

Some people really get carried away with this, but you shouldn't make the concept of matching the hatch more difficult than it has to be. Make sure that your fly box has mayfly dun imitations that represent all sizes of mayflies likely to be found in the area that you fish.

Most mayflies are represented with flies tied on hooks between sizes 12 and 20. Be sure to have light, medium, and dark shades for each size. Ideally, you should have at least a couple of each size and shade. Three of each shade, in sizes 12 to 20, would ads up to 180 mayfly dun imitations in your fly box, which can be quite an investment.

You can reduce your cash outlay by studying hatch charts, or better yet, quizzing the employees at your local fly shop to determine which fly patterns you really need, for the place and time you'll be fishing.

Whatever you do, don't ever buy just one of a fly that you think could be the hot ticket for the day. Flies are easily lost to streamside bushes and trees, bad knots, and mean fish. Imagine how you would feel if after a tough morning of fishing, and many fly changes, you finally catch a fish, only to lose your one and only "hot" fly to a tree or snag.

caddis if they get the chance. Some caddis nymphs don't make cases, but just cling to the underside of rocks and logs.

Nymphs are usually greenish, with a darker head. When a caddisfly is about to become an adult, it swims quickly to the surface, sheds its nymphal shuck and quickly flies away as an adult. Because it flies away so fast, the fish must strike quickly, or it will be too late. As a result, your adult caddis imitations don't have to be as exacting as mayfly imitations.

Stoneflies

In some streams, especially western freestone streams, stoneflies can be a very important food item. They are only found in streams with a good flow and high oxygen levels. The nymphs live on and under rocks and logs, often in extremely fast water. They have tiny claws on the end of their feet that enable them to hang onto the rocks, even in the fastest current.

Try turning over some big rocks in the middle of some rapids and you'll probably find some stoneflies. They can be quite large, up to 2 in. long, and quite fierce looking. While their backs are quite hard and dark colored, their bellies are soft and lighter in color. Fish get a chance to eat them when they lose their grip on the bottom.

Rather than swim to the surface like mayflies and caddisflies, stoneflies crawl up onto the bank when it's time for them to become adults. Once on the bank, they break out of their nymphal shuck and fly to nearby bushes to mate. You will see their many shucks on streamside rocks the day after a big emergence.

After mating, the females return to the water to lay their eggs. They buzz clumsily across the surface while doing this, and fish will feed on them with reckless abandon.

Midges

While usually quite small, midges can be present in such huge numbers that trout readily feed on them, making them of real importance to fly fishermen. The immature form of midges are, like caddisflies, referred to as larvae. They live in silt, in weeds, and under rocks and logs; in some streams they seem to be everywhere.

On some big rivers, trout will stuff themselves with them. I once caught and ate a 16-in. brown trout from the Bighorn River in Montana whose stomach looked like a stuffed sausage, and it was totally packed with tiny midge larvae.

As adults, midges look a lot like mosquitoes. They often cluster together on the surface. During a big midge hatch, the clusters can be as big as a saucer, and I've seen trout hungrily take a big bite out of the middle of a big cluster. Single midges will also be taken by fish.

The imitations are often tiny, usually size 20 to 24, and it can be difficult to have confidence in catching a fish on such a tiny hook. Keep in mind that large trout are routinely landed on these tiny flies.

These are the basics in aquatic entomology. There are many other books that go into much greater detail on this topic, but as long as you can identify what type of insect you're looking at, and which fly pattern in your box represents it the best, you'll do fine in matching the hatch.

Stonefly Nymph

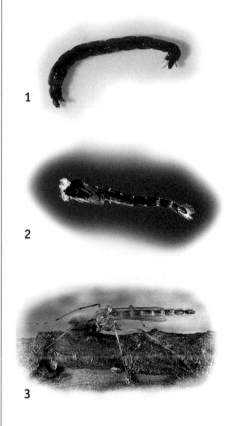

Midge Life Stages: (1) larva, (2) pupa, (3) adult.

Fly Types

Flies that imitate the various aquatic insects are typically drab in color and, in moving water, are usually drifted naturally to the fish, with little or no movement provided by the angler. Insect imitations can be divided into several categories that somewhat correspond to each insect's different stages of life. These flies are most often used for trout and panfish, but bass and other fish sometimes eat insects, too. Various styles of flies represent other possible food items.

Nymphs

Flies that imitate the nymphal forms of aquatic insects are usually tied with extra weight built into them. This is usually accomplished by wrapping lead wire on the hook shank before tying the fly.

Bead-headed nymphs are a very popular version of weighted nymphs. They sink very fast because of a brass or tungsten bead slipped onto the hook before the fly is tied. The reflective flash in the water provided by the bead adds to the attraction of this style of fly.

Some nymphs represent small crustaceans like scuds or sowbugs.

Emergers

Emergers represent the stage of aquatic insect life between larvae and adult. They can be fished below the surface to imitate a nymph swimming to the surface, or right in the surface film to imitate a nymph struggling to get out of its nymphal shuck.

Dry flies

Dry flies represent adult aquatic insects that are floating on the surface. They are often tied with bushy hackles that help them float. Dry flies must be treated with fly floatant to keep them on top of the water.

Dry flies that imitate mayflies usually have an upright wing; caddisfly and stonefly imitators have a down wing that lies along the hook shank. Midge imitations are so small that fly tiers usually don't bother with a wing.

Terrestrials

Terrestrials imitate land-born insects that are unfortunate enough to end up in the water. Wind or rain often cause bugs like beetles, ants, or grasshoppers to end up in the water. This happens often enough, especially in the summer and fall, to make them a regular part of a fish's diet.

Attractors

While most flies are tied to resemble some sort of fish food, some flies don't look like anything on Earth. (Have you ever seen something that looks like a Dardevle or a spinnerbait?) Despite their gaudy appearance, these flies can be very effective for a variety of fish.

If you were debating whether or not to eat something, you could pick it up and examine it before taking a bite. Fish don't have this ability, and will often bite something simply because it is highly visible. Attractors can fall into any of the other fly categories. For example, a Royal Wulff dry fly, a Prince nymph, and a Mickey Finn streamer are all examples of attractor flies.

Fly Types

1. Dark Hendrickson Nymph

2. Peeking Caddis

3. Giant Black Stonefly Nymph

4. Marabou Midge Larva

Nymph imitations for (1) mayfly, (2) caddisfly, (3) stonefly, and (4) midge.

1. Halo Emerger

2. Caddis Pupa

Emerger imitations for (1) mayfly and (2) caddisfly.

1. March Brown

2. Red Quill Spinner

3. Elk-hair Caddis

4. Cream Midge

Dry Fly imitations for (1) mayfly dun, (2) mayfly spinner, (3) caddisfly, and (4) midge.

1. Foam Ant

2. Black Beetle

3. Rubber Legs Henry's Fork Hopper

4. Cricket

Terrestrial imitations for (1) ant, (2) beetle, (3) grasshopper, and (4) cricket.

Streamers

Streamers are usually meant to represent minnows or other types of baitfish like perch, sculpins, or shad, and are used for any type of fish that feeds on other fish. They are often much larger than other types of flies, sometimes 5 in. long, or even bigger.

They are almost always fished below the surface, and often require action for maximum results. The wings are usually tied to move or "flow" as the fly is being retrieved.

While some streamers closely match the colors of baitfish, others are tied in bright, fluorescent colors, with flashy Mylar accents, for example. Some very effective streamers are tied with lead eyes at the front. This added weight can give the fly a jigging motion and cause the fly to ride hook point up, reducing snags on the bottom.

Leeches

All game fish eat leeches. There are several flies that represent this fish delicacy. They are tied with materials that soak up a lot of water and have good movement in the water, like marabou or rabbit fur.

These flies are usually black, brown, or olive. A wooly bugger is perhaps the best-known leech imitation, and this fly, tied in various sizes and colors, will work on all game fish.

Poppers

Poppers are one of the best known and most popular styles of flies. They can be made out of deer hair, cork, or foam, and are a favorite of bass and panfish anglers across the country. Their flat- or cupped-face design causes them to "pop" when retrieved across the surface.

They usually come with fancy paint jobs, doll eyes and rubber legs, which look great to the fishermen, but I doubt the fish care much about these details. The most important thing is that the fly makes a good popping sound!

Divers

Divers are fished in a similar manner to poppers, except that they dive just under the surface and float back up on the retrieve, rather than just chugging along like a popper. Dahlberg Divers are the best-known flies of this design. They are tied with a deer-hair head and a long flowing tail. Bass and pike find them irresistible.

Eggs

These flies are simple creations, often tied out of closely trimmed yarn. It's well known that in certain situations trout and steelhead feed actively on the eggs of salmon, or even on the eggs of other trout and steelhead.

Egg flies are usually orange or pink, and must be drifted along the bottom in order to be effective.

Attractors

Mickey Finn

Royal Wulff

Prince Nymph

Parmachene Belle Wet Fly

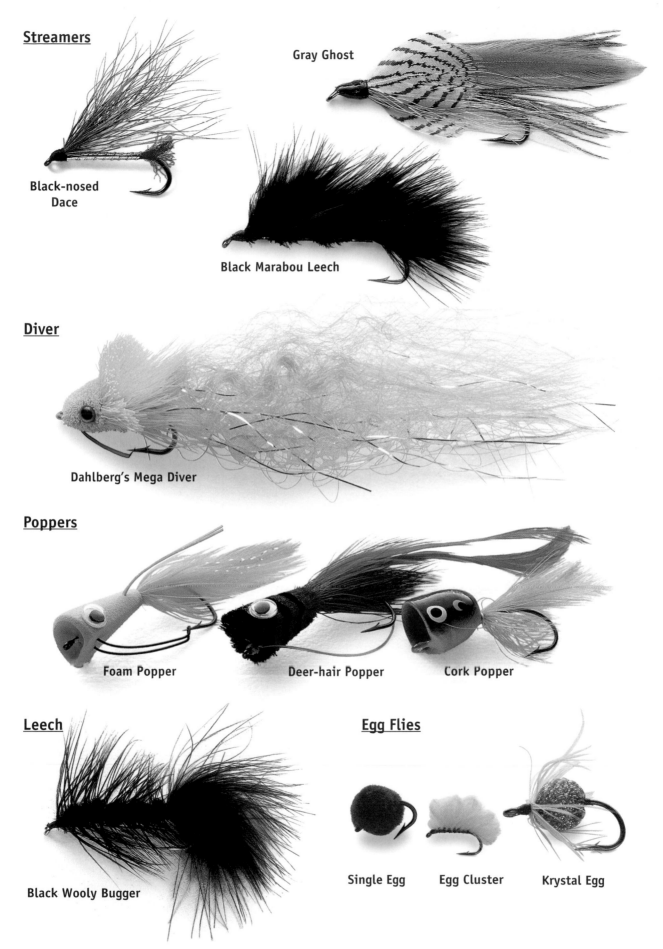

Streamers

Black-nosed Dace

Gray Ghost

Black Marabou Leech

Diver

Dahlberg's Mega Diver

Poppers

Foam Popper

Deer-hair Popper

Cork Popper

Leech

Black Wooly Bugger

Egg Flies

Single Egg

Egg Cluster

Krystal Egg

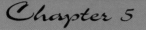

Accessories, Tackle Storage & Clothing

Whatever species of fish or type of water you will be fly fishing, there are a few basics you should have along on the outing. The number of accessories available is huge, but remember, you also need to consider where you'll keep them—on the water and at home. And choose your clothing carefully—you may fish in a variety of weather conditions.

Accessories

After you have picked out your fly-fishing outfit (rod, reel, line), it's time to accessorize. As in any sport, the list of accessories is endless. Taking a look at the accessory wall in a big fly shop can be mind boggling. With all the hook removers, strike indicators, fly floatants, leader straighteners, and much, much more, it's hard to tell what you really need.

While virtually all of the accessories available can make your fly fishing more enjoyable, it's best to start out with the basics, and add other accessories later as you need them. I consider the first six of the following to be "must haves" for any beginner.

Line cutter

You will likely be changing flies, leaders, and tippets on a regular basis, so you should have something with you to cut line and trim knots. It is important that some knots be trimmed very closely. Common options are scissors, clippers, or snippers.

I find that a scissors is the most useful of the three. Besides being able to cut line and trim knots, you can use it to doctor a fly, cut a wader patch, and many other things. Find a pair that is "tight" or stays closed when not in use. I also like a pair that isn't too pointy, for safety.

Plain old fingernail clippers also work great for cutting line and trimming knots.

Unfortunately, I have found that snippers, which are the most popular choice among fly anglers, are actually the least useful. Most snippers usually aren't sharp enough to quickly slice through leaders and tippets.

The exception is the model made by Angler's Image. These are made of stainless steel, are super sharp, and also feature a retractable needle that is used for clearing lacquer

Snipper

out of the eyes of fly hooks and untangling knots.

Hook remover

Most of the time, it is easy to get a fly out of a fish's mouth by simply backing it out by hand. This is especially true if you pinch down the barbs on your flies, as I do. Some of the time, though, you need a tool to get the hook out. If you are fishing for larger fish with big flies, a needle-nose pliers works fine.

For smaller flies, a hemostat is much better. A good pair of hemostats will enable you to extract small flies with precision, even from the back of a fish's mouth. I like the ones that have flat jaws, with no serration. The flat jaws also make it easy to flatten the barbs on your flies. All hemostats have a lock that enables you to clamp

them onto your shirt or vest when not in use.

Another style of hook remover is the Ketchum Release by Waterworks. This device enables you to pop the fly out of the fish's mouth without even touching the fish. I've been using one for a few years now, and with practice it works great, as long as you are using a barbless fly. I find them particularly useful for trout fishing in very cold weather, when wet hands can stop your fishing.

Knot-tying tool

In order to attach new leaders with a nail knot, you need some kind of tool. It is possible to tie a nail knot freehand, but I don't recommend it. Using either a Brown or Sierra knot-tying tool will make tying nail knots much easier and faster.

Hook removers.
Hemostats (left), also called forceps, are easy to use. Stainless-steel needle-nose pliers (right) work well on large flies, and they don't corrode.

All-foam fly box by Morell

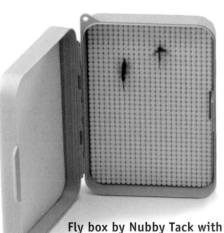

Fly box by C&F Designs with built-in fly threaders

Fly box by Nubby Tack with foam and "stick-to" panels

Fly box

Most fly boxes in use today are made of lightweight plastic. Some have compartments and some are lined with foam. Those with compartments are most useful for storing bushy flies, such as dry flies or bass bugs. Be careful when opening a compartmented box on a windy day; small dry flies can easily blow out.

Foam-lined boxes are great because you can see all of your flies at a glance, and since the flies are stuck into the foam, "blow out" isn't a problem. If you use a foam-lined box with dry flies, place them carefully in the foam to avoid crushing the hackles.

You will probably start out with only one box for all of your flies. Eventually, you should have separate boxes for each style of fly. Some fly boxes, like the ones made by Morell, are made entirely of foam. I like these a lot because they are so lightweight. Another design that has become very popular is the Fox box. While a bit heavy, the individual slots keep your flies organized and visible.

Fly boxes with built-in fly threaders are a great choice if you have trouble threading your tippet through the eye of small flies. The best of these is made by C&F Designs. You pre-load the wire loops with your flies while at home. When you want to tie one on, just poke your tippet through the wire loop and slide your fly on to it. These boxes are spendy, but they can be a real time-saver if a hatch of tiny size-20 mayflies is coming off and you really need to make a fly change.

Hook sharpener

If you fish in areas that are very rocky, your flies will likely come in contact with the rocks at some point, and become dull. This is especially common when fishing steelhead or smallmouth bass.

If you have a hook sharpener with you, you can usually resharpen a fly at least a couple times. Remember what the hook has to do: stick in the fish's mouth. You'll quickly find that fly fishing with a dull hook equals more casting practice.

For small flies, a thin file with fine serrations is best. For larger flies, a coarser file may be required.

Fly floatant

If you will be using surface, or dry flies that aren't made of a naturally buoyant material, such as cork or foam, you need a type of fly floatant.

My favorite is the kind that is made of silicone gel and comes in a small squeeze bottle. Squirt a small amount onto your fingertip and work it into all parts of the fly before the fly gets wet. Gink and Aquel are two popular and effective brands.

Fly floatant

Many anglers like the spray-bottle variety. Simply tie on your fly, and give it a good spray. Using a spray bottle avoids the problem of getting fly floatant on your fingers.

Some styles of fly floatant require that you pre-treat the fly at least a day before you plan you use it. Watershed is the best and most popular floatant of this style. Simply soak each of your dry flies with Watershed, place them on a paper towel and let them dry overnight. You don't need to do anything more to them.

No fly floatant will keep a dry fly or deer-hair bass bug floating forever. After repeated casting, and (hopefully) catching a dozen or even fewer fish, your dry fly will be waterlogged and start to sink. When this happens, you can temporarily retire the fly to dry it off, or you can apply a fly desiccant, which is made of silica crystal or powder that absorbs moisture. To use a desiccant, swish the fly in the water to rinse off any fish slime, blow off the excess water, and place your fly in the container while it is still attached to your tippet. A couple of shakes will instantly dry off your fly. You can now apply new floatant, and

Desiccant

your fly will float great again.

If your fly is too big to fit in the container, or if your desiccant doesn't come in this style of container, pour some crystals into the palm of your hand and roll the fly in them.

Fly sink

This stuff comes in a bottle similar to fly floatant. When applied to a streamer or nymph, it removes any buoyancy from the fly, causing it to sink faster.

Line cleaner

You may find that after a few fishing trips your flyline doesn't shoot out as well as it did when it was new. Giving your flyline a once-over with a good line dressing will make it shoot like new. I like the kind made by Scientific Anglers the best.

No amount of cleaning or dressing, however, will make a line float better. Flylines float because of microscopic air bubbles in the line. Eventually, these bubbles will break, and your line will start to sink. You can either put up with a line that sinks, or get a new one.

Split shot/weight

Sometimes you need to add a little extra weight to your fly to get it down. Small split shot can easily be added to your leader, and removed when you don't need them anymore. I usually use Water Gremlin removable split shot, size B, but they can be hard to find. Most fly shops sell round split shot that come in a dispenser that holds several sizes. In these dispensers, you'll find that the #4 size shot is the most useful.

Another way to add extra weight to your leader is by using one of several moldable

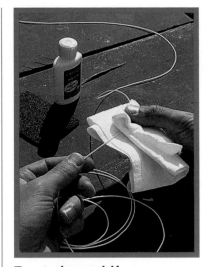

Treat cleaned line with a protectant to maintain the plastic coating and help the line shoot smoothly through the guides.

Types of weights I recommend include split shot (left) and moldable (right).

Strike indicators for nymph fishing come in many varieties. Some of my favorites are (from top to bottom): yarn, Corky, foam adhesive, and strike putty.

Retractor

weight products available. Shape-a-Wate and Loon Deep Soft Weight are two good examples. While not as heavy as split shot, moldable weights don't snag up as much and are easier to cast. Moldable weight stays in place best if you put it right on top of a tippet knot.

Strike indicator

Strike indicators are used when nymph fishing in streams. While they can be used to suspend your fly above the bottom like a bobber, most fly anglers use them as a visual aid to track the progress of their fly.

Leader straightener

Leader straighteners are rubber pads covered with leather. When you open a leader package, you'll find that the tapered leader is quite tightly coiled. By drawing the leader through these pads, all the coils are taken out. You can straighten a leader by hand, by pulling hard on it at 2-ft. intervals, but a leader straightener is easier to use. A leader straightener also takes the shine off the finish of your leader; a "dull" leader is less likely to spook fish.

Retractor

Many of the tools and accessories that you need are best hung on retractors. They keep the tools out of the way, held tightly against your vest until you need them. Some are spring-loaded, and some have a pigtail cord, like a phone cord. The pigtail kinds are much less likely to break, but don't always retract as smoothly as the spring-loaded kind.

Fly patch

Fly patches are pinned onto your vest and used to temporarily store flies, especially water-logged dry flies. They can be made of fleece or foam. Some of the newer foam models are made of a super-dense foam that will hold even barbless hooks. If you put flies in any kind of a fly patch, keep in mind that none of the designs are perfect, and some flies may fall out and become lost.

Instead of a fly patch, you may want to consider the Fly Trap by Waterworks. It is a small, ventilated fly box that you wear on the outside of your vest. Flies placed in here will not be lost while they dry. Also, by keeping a few of your favorite flies in a fly trap instead of in a box in a vest pocket, you can access and change flies much more quickly.

Flashlight

If you plan on fishing until dark, a small flashlight can be a great help in making the last few fly changes of the day, and help you find your way back to the parking lot. If you expect that you will be a ways from your vehicle, carry a second, larger flashlight as well.

After a couple of incidents where I had a tough time finding and staying on the trail back to my truck, I now always keep a two-D-cell flashlight in my vest for evening sessions.

Thermometer

There are times when it is important to know what the temperature of the water is. All fish have a preferred temperature range to live in, and checking the water temp will give you an idea of what the fish's activity level will be.

Tape measure

We all like to know how big the fish we catch are. Having a tape measure gives you the ability to know exactly how big your fish are. How much you exaggerate is between you and your conscience!

Landing net

To increase the odds of landing the fish you hook, you may want to carry a landing net with you. Make sure that your net is big enough to hold the biggest fish you could ever expect to catch. I chuckle whenever I see someone on a trout stream with a net the size of a ping-pong paddle. A little net will scoop up a 10" trout okay, but what if you hook up to a 20 incher?

The down side to carrying nets is that they are always getting tangled in the brush. So, if you're going to the trouble of carrying a net with you, make sure it is big enough.

If you have a good net release attached to the back of your vest, carrying a landing

net is less of a hassle. The models made by Rosecreek and the Mayfly Company both work great. They hold the net with the hoop up, which helps keep the net bag out of the bushes.

If you'll be fishing from a boat, you may want to have a net with a longer handle than those used by stream fishermen.

Whatever style of net you decide on, make sure that the bag is made of soft mesh. Hard-nylon net bags are really damaging to fish because they remove slime and scales.

Magnifier

If you find that you have problems tying knots, a small magnifier may be a tremendous help, especially in low light or whenever small flies are being used. Flip-Focals are one of the best and easiest varieties to use. You clip them onto the brim of your hat, where they are folded out of the way until you need them.

Tippet holder

This is used to store a few spools of your favorite sizes of tippet material on the outside of your vest where they can be easily accessed.

Lanyard

Some anglers like to hang their tools and accessories on a lanyard around their neck. They usually have between four and eight clips to hang things on. Be sure to get one with a clip on the bottom. You attach this clip to your shirt to keep the necklace from swinging all over the place.

Multi-tool

What a great invention. Leatherman and Gerber both offer models for fly anglers. I favor the Gerber Compact Sport—I don't leave home without mine. This model, besides featuring a needle-nose pliers that can be opened with one hand, also has a scissors, can opener, bottle opener, wire cutter, knife, and several screwdrivers. If you have one, you'll find that you use it almost every time you go fishing.

Things to Remember When Buying Accessories

• Buy the best quality of tools and accessories you can afford.

• When wearing a vest, hang often-used accessories on retractors.

• Having extras of frequently used tools is a good idea in case of loss.

• Don't hang too many things on the outside of your vest; they can get in the way.

Tackle Storage

How you keep all your tackle organized and easily accessible depends on whether you will be fishing mainly from a boat or wading, and on your own personal preferences.

In a boat, you'll have plenty of room for a tackle box or tackle bag. So pack them up to your heart's content!

If you will be wading, carrying them with you isn't practical. Since you'll be out in the water most of the time, you would have to return to shore every time you needed something out of your tackle box or bag.

Vests are the most obvious and popular choice for tackle storage while wading, but there are other options available that may better suit your needs or tastes.

Vests

People have been wearing fly-fishing vests for almost as long as people have been fly fishing. There is no better way to keep all of your flies and accessories organized while wading than with a well-designed vest. Most vests have between fifteen and twenty-five separate pockets. You may think that you don't need all those pockets, and at first, you won't. As you add more fly boxes and other accessories to your arsenal, you'll be glad that your vest has ample storage.

Vests are available in many styles with many different pocket arrangements, as well as in many different price points. A good vest should last you a minimum of ten years.

Most vests are designed to hang down to just above your waist. And they work just fine for most anglers.

Full-length vests hang down a bit farther. Because they are longer, there's more room for pockets, so storage space is increased. The pockets on these vests ride lower, so the top pockets are easier to get at. The downside of this vest style is that it can be hard to keep the bottom of it out of the water. Even if you never plan on wading out waist-deep, you still may get the bottom of your vest soaked if you kneel down into the water to release a fish.

Shorty vests are popular with anglers who constantly find themselves wading deep. The smaller overall size reduces storage space, though, and you'll find that the top pockets are right up at your shoulders and a bit hard to get at easily.

Be sure to get a vest that

fits properly. Always try on the vest over as much clothing as you think you'll ever wear, including a rain jacket. When in doubt, err on the large side to account for vest shrinkage (or angler expansion).

Your vest should have a large pocket on the back. It should be large enough to hold a rain jacket or sweater, as well as other items such as a water bottle or lunch.

Some vests are better for hot weather than others. If keeping cool is a big concern, you should consider getting an open-mesh vest. The fabric will ensure that you won't get hot because of your vest. However, the open mesh is more likely to get caught in streamside bushes than vests made of solid material.

Some anglers wear vests that are dark colored or camouflaged (such as those made by Aqua Designs), to blend in with their surroundings. I fish on a lot of small, clear trout streams where approaching your spot without being detected by the fish is a big part of being successful. Under these conditions, blending in with your surroundings can't be a bad thing. Beware that the dark fabric will soak up a lot of heat on hot, sunny days.

The vest fabric can also influence your comfort level while fishing. Cotton is a very popular choice. It is a very durable, natural material that "breathes," keeping you relatively cool on hot days.

Vests made of nylon, while a bit warm on hot summer days, are very durable. In my opinion, the best-designed vest available is the Simms Guide Vest. It is constructed of a nylon/poly blend with a mesh lining. The lining helps to keep the wearer

comfortable when it's hot. The price is high (around $150), but all the pockets are the right size and in the right places. I know it will be many years before I wear mine out. Of course there are other quality vests available at lower prices. Redington and Columbia both offer good vests for between $50 and $100.

While not technically a vest, a waterproof jacket designed for fly fishing can function as a vest does in rainy weather. The Simms Guide Coat or Redington's Q-Nimbus are among the best. For rainy or cold days, skip the vest or pack and put your essential gear in the pockets of a jacket.

Chest packs

Some anglers find that they just don't need the storage space of a vest. If you consider yourself to be a "fair-weather fisherman," or only plan to fish for short sessions, a chest pack may be a good choice for you. Chest packs are designed to hold a couple of fly boxes and the essential tools and accessories.

It seems that chest packs are gaining in popularity, particularly in the western U.S., but I doubt they will ever replace vests. The only way to know if a chest pack is right for you is to try one.

Hip/fanny packs

For the real minimalist, or for short trips, a hip or fanny pack

can be just the ticket. These packs usually have only enough room for one fly box and basic tools and accessories.

In hot weather, especially where no deep wading is required, or when you'll only be out for a short time, you might find one of these packs to be a nice complement to the vest you normally wear.

If you really like the idea of a hip or fanny pack, wearing a lightweight fishing shirt with large pockets at the same time will increase your storage space.

Tackle bags

So far, I have described tackle storage for wading anglers. People often associate fly fishing exclusively with wading, but fly fishing in some places requires angling from a boat. While any of the previously mentioned tackle storage options will work for angling from a boat, you can skip wearing a vest or pack by keeping all your fly-fishing gear in a tackle bag. Any small duffel bag will work, but bags that are made especially for fly anglers work the best. With a fly fishing tackle bag, you can quickly find what you're looking for.

Tackle bags are usually water resistant, and built to last. The Holds Everything bag by Abel is the best-known bag of this style; Sage, Redington, and others also offer bags of similar design.

Most have several outside pockets, as well as dividers and additional pockets on the inside. Even if you don't fish from a boat, you might find one of these bags to be helpful in keeping your tackle organized when not in use.

Fly fishing tackle bags are also the perfect size to be used as an airplane carry-on bag.

Rod cases

When your fly rod isn't in use, it's a good idea to store it in some kind of hard case. Most quality fly rods come with a case, either aluminum or cordura-covered PVC. Most fly

shops sell fly-rod cases if your rod didn't come with one.

If you don't store your rod in a case, you're just asking for trouble. Even though your rod may come with a great warranty, that won't do you any good when you get to the stream only to find that it has been broken in transit. If you have an aluminum case, you should put your rod in a cloth rod bag first to keep it from rattling around inside. Most PVC cases have a nylon divider inside to keep your rod sections secure.

Fly-rod cases are available in several diameters. If your rod is a two piece, a 1⅝-in. case should be big enough, unless it has unusually large components. A 2-in. rod case is large enough to hold all other rods, including four- or five-piece models.

You can easily make your own rod case out of PVC plumbing pipe. Go to a home supply store and buy a length of 2-in. diameter pipe, along with a cap for one end and a screw-cap for the other. Cut the pipe to length, glue the ends on, and you've got a very durable (although quite ugly) rod case. One nice thing about using this style of case is that it doesn't really look like a fly-rod case to would-be thieves.

There are also many fly-rod

cases available that enable you to store your rod with the reel still attached. These cases are made of cordura-covered PVC with a zippered padded pouch at the top. While not quite as dependable as straight rod tubes, their convenience has made them a favorite storage option. You can even store your rod strung up inside the case with a fly tied on, if you do it right!

Store your rod in a secure rod tube.

Popular styles include: (1) aluminum with screw-on cap; (2) plastic; (3) cordura with PVC interior tube; (4) multirod; and (5) rod-and-reel style, for packing your fly rod with reel attached.

Clothing

I am amazed at how many people will dress to be comfortable most of the time, such as for work or shopping, but are willing to be uncomfortable when they're fishing. You're supposed to be having fun out there, right? So why suffer by being too hot or too cold when you could buy great clothing designed for anglers. Some of this specialty clothing comes with a hefty price tag, but so do business suits. And you rarely have any fun while wearing a business suit!

Cold weather

Anyone who lives in a cold climate has heard by now how important it is to dress in layers. While old advice, it is still true. By wearing the right layers, you can stay warm in any weather. A couple layers of the right clothing is far better than many layers of the wrong clothing. If you put on too many layers, however, your freedom of movement will be compromised.

Start out by wearing good-quality long underwear, such as products made by Simms or Patagonia. Do not wear cotton long underwear or a T-shirt and expect to stay warm. Cotton is comfortable in warm weather, but a very poor insulator when compared with synthetic fabrics like polyester or Capilene. When hiking to a stream or lake, you can't help but sweat a little, even in cold weather. Cotton long underwear will hold this moisture against your skin, and it won't be long until you're cold. Long underwear of the proper fabric will actually wick the moisture away from you. Long underwear designed for anglers even has stirrups to prevent it from riding up your legs when you pull on other layers.

Your second layer should be fleece pants on the bottom and a fleece jacket on the top. (Fleece dries very quickly.) I find two pairs of fleece pants necessary if I'm wearing lightweight waders in very cold water, especially if I'm wading deep.

If you're a traditionalist, you can substitute a wool sweater for the fleece jacket.

Wool is definitely also my material of choice for socks, especially merino wool. Wool is very comfortable in all weather conditions, and keeps you warm even when wet.

After you have your waders on, add a wading jacket, ideally a breathable one, to cut the wind. I have fished many times in sub-freezing temperatures with an outfit like the one I just described and stayed warm enough to fish all day.

The weak link in cold-weather fishing is your hands. I have worn every style of fishing glove available, and have found the best to be wind-proof fleece, fingerless gloves that

have a fold-over mitten flap. I've even worn this style of glove when ice fishing. When I'm fishing, I keep the flaps folded back out of the way. When I need to warm up my hands, I fold the flaps back in place over my fingers. If the gloves get wet—and they will—you can wring or shake the water out of them and continue wearing them. Keeping a second pair of dry gloves in the back of your vest will enable you to keep fishing if the first pair gets really soaked.

I always keep a few disposable handwarmers in my vest or jacket on cold days. You can slip one right inside your glove, and it will really speed up the warming process.

When I'm fishing, I almost always wear a baseball cap. Even in cold weather I can keep my head warm by putting up the hood on my wading jacket. On very cold days, though, I usually

opt for the added warmth of a wool Elmer Fudd or stocking cap.

Warm weather

Dressing properly for warm weather is much easier than dressing for cold weather. Keep in mind that even though the air temperature may feel warm, the water may be much cooler. So if you'll be wading, you still may want to wear fleece pants under your waders. If you know the water temp will be warm, a pair of lightweight pants will do nicely. (I've never liked wearing shorts under waders.)

For a shirt, almost anything will work, even a T-shirt. A lightweight fishing shirt with long sleeves is what you will almost always see me wearing on warm days, though. I can roll the sleeves up on hot days, and keep them down on cooler days or when I've gotten enough sun. Shirt fabric can be cotton, nylon, or a blend of the two. Cotton is

the best for really hot days, but the nylon shirts designed for fishing often have UV blockers built in, so if you burn easily, you won't have to worry. Tarponwear is the best-known manufacturer of this style of shirt. Nylon shirts also dry very quickly, and are relatively wrinkle free.

You should always wear a hat, whether it's cold or hot. A baseball hat is the obvious choice. Be sure to wear one that is dark on the underside of the bill, so that light reflecting off the surface of the water will be absorbed by the dark color. Do not wear your baseball hat backward—that defeats the whole purpose of the protection of your face from the brim. If you are very sensitive to the sun, wearing a flats-style hat is a good idea. These versions have a large flap that goes all the way around the back to protect your ears and neck from the sun.

If you really spend a lot of

time in the sun, you may want to wear a pair of sunblocker gloves. They are very lightweight and will reduce the need to put sunblock on your hands or wrists.

A good sunblock is something that most people should put on whenever fishing in the summertime. Backcountry Laboratories makes a great sunblock that is waterproof and not too greasy, and doesn't have a strong odor.

Polarized sunglasses

Polarized sunglasses are really mandatory equipment for all kinds of fishing. For one thing, they are great protection from hooks! For another, they reduce the glare from the surface of the water, enabling you to see into the water.

I got my first pair when I was about ten. At that time, there wasn't the variety of styles that is available now, so my first pair was huge on my face. They did the job, though, even though they made me look like a miniature Roy Orbison.

You can find polarized sunglasses in many locations, in a wide price range. Remember, though, you get what you pay for; better-quality models give the best protection.

The lenses of polarized sunglasses can be made of several different materials:

• Plastic lenses are found in cheap sunglasses. They really don't have great optical quality, and things sometimes look distorted through them. They also scratch very easily. But cheap ones are better than no sunglasses at all.

• Polycarbonate lenses are usually found in medium-priced sunglasses. Polycarbonate is somewhat scratch resistant, and the optical quality of the lenses is better than plastic. Polycarbonate lenses are also very impact resistant. Another advantage of polycarbonate lenses is that they are very lightweight, so they are comfortable.

• Glass lenses give you the best optical quality—everything looks sharper and clearer. Glass lenses are very scratch resistant, and a good pair will last for many years. The only bad thing about glass lenses is that they are heavier than other styles, so if you get a pair that doesn't fit your face right, you can have a problem with them sliding down your nose.

Action Optics makes a high-quality pair of sunglasses.

Polarized sunglasses are available with several different lens colors. Different colors of lenses work best in different conditions:

• Yellow lenses are great for low-light periods or dark, overcast days. They don't cut out much light, so you don't want to have them for your only pair. They actually seem to make everything look somewhat brighter, a big plus on dark days.

• Gray lenses are usually on the other end of the darkness spectrum. They cut out the most light, often too much. For very bright days, they are a good choice, but they don't give you the contrast that enables you to make out underwater features as well as brown or copper lenses do.

• Brown or copper lenses are the choice of most anglers, fly and otherwise. They are dark, but not too dark, and give good contrast for spotting fish, weed beds, and other underwater features.

Many companies offer high-quality polarized sunglasses. I highly recommend the Action Optics brand, which come in a wide variety of frame designs with polycarbonate or glass lenses.

You should have some kind of lanyard on your sunglasses, such as the models by Croakies or Chumms. With a lanyard, you can let the glasses hang around your neck when you want to take them off. Otherwise, you'll be setting them down somewhere, putting them in a pocket, or wearing them on top of your head, inviting breakage or loss.

Things to Remember When Buying Clothing

• Poly, fleece, and wool are good for cold weather.

• Cotton and nylon are good for hot weather.

• Loose is better tight.

• Bring an assortment of clothing with you—for all weather conditions.

• Inexpensive polarized sunglasses are better than expensive, designer non-polarized ones.

• Photochromatic lenses, which lighten and darken with the conditions, are pricey, but handy to have.

Chapter 6

Waders, Tubes & Watercraft

Fly fishing will always require that you get near or actually in the water. Some fishing is best done from a type of watercraft, but the ability to have a fun day of fishing without the hassles of a boat is one of the many appeals of fly fishing.

Waders

There are many different materials and styles of waders available, and trying to make a decision can be difficult. Here are a few tips to make it easier:

Hip boots

The first choice for a new fly fisherman is often hip boots. They seem so simple—easy to put on and take off—and who needs to wade in up to your chest anyway? If all your fishing will be on small streams, where you will never need to be in water more than a foot deep, hip boots may be a good choice.

In my early days of stream fishing I started out wearing hip boots. Unfortunately, sometimes the water ended up being an inch over the top of my boots, and I ended up with wet feet. Another negative of hippers is that you have to watch where you sit down along the stream to avoid getting the seat of your pants wet or dirty.

Chest-high Waders expand your fishing range by allowing you to wade deeper. Using a wading belt ensures your waders won't fill with water if you should fall.

Chest-high waders

These are the most popular choice with fly fishermen, whether they fish streams or lakes. While it is rare (and not recommended) that you need to wade in deeper than your hips, it's nice to have the ability to make a deep stream crossing, or to get out far enough from shore to get some backcast room. Chest waders allow you to sit down on any riverbank without soiling your clothes; if it's raining, you'll never get wet with the right rain jacket.

If you decide to get chest waders, you'll need to choose between boot-foot and stocking-foot versions. Each style has its advantages.

• Boot-foot waders are ready to wear. They are easy and fast to put on, and there are fewer pieces to keep track of. Also, in cold water, boot-foots are warmer because they fit more loosely, allowing for better circulation and more layers of clothing.

Because they are looser fitting, they are a bit bulky, so they can be tiring for walking long distances. They also don't give you much ankle support.

• Stocking-foot waders are a bit more of a hassle to put on and take off because they require the use of separate wading boots over the waders. After pulling the waders on, you have to put on your wading shoes, lace them up and then put on gravel guards. Once you have done this, though, you will be far more sure-footed than would be possible in boot-foots, whether you're hiking in or crossing the stream.

When you lace up that wading shoe, it's like lacing up a hiking boot, so you have great ankle support. You'll really appreciate

Hip boots work well in relatively shallow water.

this ankle support when wading in a rocky stream. Stocking-foots are usually snugger fitting, which makes for easier walking. And you'll be more streamlined in the water, a plus in fast current.

Material

Now you have to decide what material your waders will be made of. If you haven't shopped for waders lately, you probably envision some pre-historic rubber creations your grandpa wore duck hunting. Modern waders are usually made of either neoprene or some breathable, waterproof material like Gore-Tex. All quality wader companies offer their waders in a wide range of sizes to fit any angler, male or female.

• Neoprene waders are made of a material similar to a scuba diver's wet suit, except that neoprene waders are waterproof. Neoprenes are very durable, and can stand up to a lot of brush busting. If you should get a leak in them, they are easy to patch with products like Aquaseal or Sun-Set Super Patch.

If you plan on doing some fly fishing in very cold weather, and especially if you will be wading in deep, cold water, neoprenes will keep you warmer than other wader materials.

• The current rage in waders is breathables. This innovation was first introduced in the early nineties. Unfortunately, with only a few exceptions, they leaked. The manufacturers have come a long way in the last ten years in improving the quality and durability of breathables.

When you think about it, how can you go wrong buying waders that are waterproof but allow moisture to escape, even underwater? Breathable waders are generally quite a bit more expensive than neoprenes.

When wearing breathable waders, you'll stay dry and comfortable, even on hot days. In cold weather, you can stay warm if you dress properly under your breathables, but probably not as warm as in neoprenes.

I live in Minnesota, where temperatures vary greatly from season to season. Standing in a 35-degree steelhead river in March requires the use of different waders than in an eighty-degree bass lake in August. I find that I wear waders as much in cold weather as in hot, so I have several pairs of waders to meet a wide variety of conditions. Buying both neoprene and lightweight breathable stocking-foot waders and a pair of wading shoes will ensure that you are comfortable, no matter the weather.

Fit

To be sure that your waders fit properly, buy them where you can try them on first. Boot-foots are usually sized by shoe size, with the body size of the waders increasing proportionately as the shoe size goes up. Stocking-foots are sized by body size (medium, large, large stout, extra large tall, etc.). It is usually easier to find a good fit in stocking-foots than in boot-foots.

If buying neoprenes, remember that the material is stretchy, so your waders should be fairly snug. Breathable waders aren't stretchy, so they have to be a little baggy to allow freedom of movement. Be sure that your waders allow enough room to allow climbing over obstacles, or squatting down. Whatever style of waders you get, too big is better than too small.

If you decide to get stocking-foot waders, you also have to get some wading shoes. Again, you should buy them where you can try them on first. Wading

Stocking-foot vs. Boot-foot waders

Which style of wader you choose is a matter of personal preference. Stocking-foots (left) require a separate wading boot, but are more confortable for walking, with good ankle support. However, the loose fit of boot-foots (right) makes them easier to put on and remove.

shoes are sized like other shoes, but you will probably find you need to go up at least one size from your normal shoe size to get a good fit. (I wear a 9½ street shoe, but a size 11 wading boot is usually what fits me best.) You'll have to trust me on this one, but having your wading shoes be a little loose is much better than too tight. Tight wading shoes will guarantee that you will get cold feet. Also, wading shoes tend to shrink over time, so starting out with them a little big is a good idea.

Soles

The soles of wading shoes and boot-footed waders are available in felt or rubber-cleated styles. In almost all wading situations, felt is the way to go. Felt soles really grab onto the bottom of the lake or stream, cutting through the moss and algae that covers the rocks. Rubber soles tend to slide along the bottom, so stumbles are inevitable.

Do yourself a favor and get felts. You'll be happy with how much more traction you get compared with rubber soles.

If you plan on fishing in areas that are very rocky, and especially if there's strong current, felt soles with metal studs are the best of all. These shoes give you unbeatable traction. The only downside to studs is that they can damage the floors of boats and float planes—and homes.

Wading shoes like the Chota feature screw-in studs that give you the ability to have studded shoes, and remove the studs in certain situations. I have worn these shoes for a year now, and they work great. Besides being awesome for wading in fast streams, the studs are a great help for gripping steep banks when climbing in or out of the stream, and for climbing over streamside logs.

Warm-weather anglers may find they can get by without any waders at all. Wet wading can be a lot of fun, and a great way to cool off on a hot summer day. When I plan on wet wading, I wear either a pair of shorts or lightweight pants. I still wear my felt-soled wading shoes, and I put them on over a pair of neoprene socks, which cut down on the amount of sand and grit that gets in against my feet. If you will have to walk through tall weeds or brush to get to the water, lightweight pants will give you some protection. On streams with very cold water, like spring creeks or some tailwater rivers, the water may be too cold to wet wade even on the hottest days. And you'll be thankful you have a good pair of waders!

Types of Wading Soles

Wader sole materials: Lug soles (above) offer good traction on muddy banks and streambeds. They are a poor choice, however, for slippery streambeds or fast water. Felt soles (top right) grip well on mossy rocks and in moderately fast water. Studded soles (bottom right) provide maximum wading traction. They are ideal for swift or slippery-bottomed streams.

Wading Tips

I've been wading in streams and lakes my whole life. I've taken a few spills over the years, but for the most part, crossing a stream isn't much more difficult for me than crossing the street. This is because I'm used to dealing with slippery stream bottoms and current, and I always wear the proper wading gear.

If you haven't waded before, walking on slippery rocks in current can be quite a challenge. Falling in means that at the very least, you will be soaking wet. You could also suffer an injury or worse.

Here are some tips that will make becoming a proficient wader easy and safe.

Fit

Wear waders that fit properly, and make sure they have felt soles.

Some waders come with a wading belt. If yours didn't, get one. Belts don't cost much, and are an important item to wear. If you should fall into deep water, your waders would quickly fill up with water. A wading belt around your waist helps keep the water out. It can also be a handy place to hang a pair of pliers, a landing net, or a wading staff.

Wading staff

If you're unsure of your wading ability, or if you're wading in unfamiliar waters, a wading staff can be a lifesaver. The best ones collapse into small sections and fit in a holster. When extended, they look and function like a walking stick. Some of the best ones are made by Simms and Folstaf. They aren't cheap, but you don't need a wading staff until you *really need* a wading staff.

A wading staff will not only give you added stability when crossing a stream, but you can use it to probe ahead of you to check for obstacles or water depth.

Crossing streams

When crossing a stream, keep your center of gravity to the rear by sliding each foot out to make a step. By doing this, your feet will bump into any wading obstacles before they become a hazard.

• The first thing to remember is to always face the bank that you are heading to. Never face directly up-stream or down-stream. If you do, you double the amount of surface area the current can push against.

On one of my first steelhead fishing trips I got myself into a tough spot while making a deep crossing. As I got farther across the stream, the water kept getting deeper. I started to panic when the water became waist high.

I started to turn around, but that caused me to be facing right into the current, and the current was really pushing against me. I was afraid to move in any direction.

The fact that I was wearing bulky, boot-foot rubber waders with rubber soles didn't help matters.

Luckily for me, another steelheader was crossing behind me. This guy was huge, and he just grabbed me by the vest and hauled me the rest of the way

Whether fishing or leaving the water, position yourself crosswise to the flow of the water, for safety.

across the river.

• Try to cross a stream in a shallow spot with a firm bottom. On a small stream, this isn't much of a factor, but on bigger water, choose your crossing wisely. On streams that receive a lot of pressure, there are usually paths along the river. If the path you are walking on disappears into the river, that's a clue that this is a good crossing spot. In places like this, the trail usually continues on the other side of the river.

• Some slow-moving streams have a lot of silt or muck in the shallows along the bank. It can be alarming to step into what appears to be a only a few inches of water, only to sink in up to your knees in muck. When this happens to me, I find the best thing to do is to keep moving, and head toward the center of the stream, where the current keeps the riverbed clear of silt. If you decide to get back out (often

a good idea), again, keep moving and head back to dry land.

• The best crossing spots on larger streams are usually found just upstream of a riffle or rapids. When the water is discolored from runoff, it can be more difficult to know where it is safe to cross. Proceed with caution under these conditions, using your wading staff to check the water depth as you go. Wherever you cross, try to move at a downstream angle.

• Crossing a fast-flowing stream is always easier with a buddy. To use the buddy system, have the stronger wader on the upstream side. Grab on to each other's vest and proceed across with the stronger wader taking the first step, and the other following. Take it slow, one step at a time.

The second wader shouldn't take a step until the first wader has his or her feet firmly planted, and vice versa. Two anglers

together can easily, although slowly, cross in the fastest current this way.

• This may sound strange, but you can actually use your fly rod to help steady yourself while crossing a stream. If you are crossing water that is over knee deep, have your fly rod in the hand that is on the downstream side. If you stick your rod just into the water in front of you and pull upstream on it, the force of the current against the rod provides enough resistance for you to lean on it. I have saved myself from a dunking on several occasions by doing this. Be careful not to stick your rod too far under the water, though. You could easily break it if you jam it into a rock.

Falling

It is inevitable that at some point you will stumble while wading and fall in. Of course, you shouldn't panic—but you probably will, especially if you're in fast or deep water. Once you get past the panic stage, try to swim to the closest shallow water, usually where you came from. Keep your feet facing downstream while you swim against the current to regain control.

Once you've dragged yourself out and checked to see if anyone saw your blunder, take off your waders and dump out the water. You should also wring out as much water from your clothing as possible. If it isn't too cold, you can keep fishing. If you're wearing Gore-Tex breathable waders, your clothes will actually dry while you fish, even underwater.

I always have at least one set of dry clothes in my truck in case of such a mishap. It's nice to have dry clothes for the ride home.

Watercraft

While it is possible to fly fish out of any watercraft, certain kinds have proven to be very popular with fly anglers.

Float tubes

Float tubes are round or U-shaped bladders covered with a nylon shell, with a seat in the middle. I have spent many hours fishing from a float tube (or belly boat). For a variety of reasons, tubes are ideal for fly fishing in lakes and ponds.

If your lake fishing has been limited to the waters you can wade, imagine now having the freedom to fish the whole lake with a minimal investment. Since you move yourself around with your legs, you can maintain your position and cast at the same time—a big plus on windy days.

Compared to other styles of boats, float tubes are inexpensive, with top-of-the-line models selling for around $200, and plenty of models available for around $100.

They are very easy to transport. I really like being able to transport my watercraft without the hassles of using a boat trailer. When deflated, tubes fit easily into a medium-size duffel bag. When inflated, they fit into the back of most pickups or SUVs, and even into the backseat of large cars.

Over the years, I've gathered a few inflation tips:

• Some float tubes are doughnut-shaped. You can get them with either a lightweight urethane bladder or with an actual rubber inner tube for a bladder. Finding a float tube that comes with an inner tube

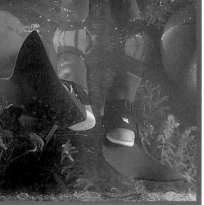

Float tubes are a great way to fly fish. They are lightweight and easy to carry. Because you use kick fins to propel yourself, float tubes are also very quiet on the water.

is becoming difficult, but the Trout Traps Company offers a variety of inflatable boats, including some with inner tubes.

- An inner tube is durable and holds its volume of air well. A lightweight bladder can lose some of its volume when you put it into a cool lake.

- The negatives of inner tubes are that they are heavier and take longer to inflate. I usually inflate mine with a compressor at a gas station, which only takes a couple of minutes. Portable compressors that plug into the cigarette lighter in your vehicle also work great. They take about ten minutes to inflate a tube, but you can use this time to string up your rod and put on your waders.

- I've inflated an inner tube with a bicycle tire pump before, and it takes about 500 pumps (I've counted!). So if you plan on fishing lakes where pumping up your tube on location will be required, a lightweight bladder is the better choice. A double-action hand pump will inflate a lightweight bladder in only a couple of minutes. Tubes with lightweight bladders also pack down smaller and weigh less than those with inner tubes.

- Be sure to inflate your tube to the proper level. Many first-time float tubers are afraid to put enough air into their tube. When you're done inflating, your tube should be almost rock hard, like a basketball. If you don't put enough air in your tube, you'll ride very low in the water, and end your day thinking that float tubing is greatly overrated.

Don't leave your tube fully inflated inside a vehicle on a warm day. The air inside the

Safety Tips When Using Float Tubes

Despite what you may think, float tubes are actually very safe to use, as long as you follow some common-sense safety rules.

1. A round float tube is almost impossible to tip over in a lake because your center of gravity is so low. I used mine on Lake Michigan in 4-ft. waves once (only once, though!), and I never felt in any danger.

2. And since the air pressure inside the tube is only 2 to 3 PSI, if you somehow got a major leak, it would take at least 5 or 10 minutes for the tube to deflate, giving you plenty of time to get to shore. I was float-tubing on a small lake once when my tube developed a pinhole leak. While the fizzing sound was distracting, I still fished for another couple hours. All quality tubes have at least one back-up air chamber, in the form of a backrest.

3. It goes without saying that you should always wear a life vest while float tubing.

4. Never use your float tube in areas with heavy boating traffic, and even in areas with light boating traffic, be sure to have some fluorescent colors showing. Most tubes have some blaze orange showing at the top.

5. Don't ever try to use a float tube, especially a round one, in a river or stream. In a round tube, too much of your body hangs underwater, and you could get caught on an obstruction. There are other types of watercraft designed for moving water.

6. Always wear waders, and be sure to wear enough warm clothes under them. Even on a warm day, being half-submerged in a cool lake for several hours can give you a chill.

tube will expand and can blow out the seams of the cover. (It's happened to me.)

And here are some tips on using a tube:

- A round tube can be tricky to get in and out of. At least on your first couple of trips, launch at a spot with a sand or gravel bottom that drops off gradually.

- Some anglers prefer open-ended or U-boats over traditional round tubes. The biggest advantage of U-boats is the fact that they are so easy to get in and out of; you just push it out into the water and sit down. Also, because your legs hang straight back you can go

through shallow or weedy water more easily than in a round tube. U-boats are available only with a lightweight bladder.

- While you'll never be able to quickly cover a lot of water from a float tube, the water that you do fish can be worked very thoroughly. Fish aren't alarmed by an angler in a float tube, because you're so low to the water, and the tube is so quiet.

- You propel a float tube by using fins on your feet. While any swim fins will work, the ones designed for tubing are the best. Force Fins are the best and everyone I fish with uses

them. But with their hefty price tag, many float tubers opt for less expensive but practical fins like those made by Trout Traps or Caddis. With any of these fins, you propel yourself backward. Don't believe any ads you see for fins that enable you to propel yourself forward. They just don't work.

Pontoon boats

No, not the kind your grandparents keep at their lake cabin. The pontoon boats I'm referring to are designed for fly anglers. They consist of two pontoons, usually between 5 ft. and 10 ft. long, held together by an aluminum frame with a seat in the middle. A pontoon boat is propelled by oars, but using fins will help you stay in position while fishing. Use the oars to get to the area you plan to fish, then use your fins while actually fishing.

This style of boat has really become popular in the last few years. While not as easy to transport or store as float tubes, pontoon boats do offer a few big advantages. The best thing about them is that they are great for floating rivers. They float in only a couple of inches of water, and are very maneuverable when you use the oars. Most of the larger pontoon boats come with a rear cargo deck that can carry enough gear for an extended trip. If you plan on floating a river, you have to plan ahead. If you decide to get

a pontoon boat for floating rivers, you should convince a friend to buy one as well. It's a lot easier to set up a float trip if there are two of you.

Pontoon boats are also great for fishing on lakes. By rowing, you can reach distant hot spots relatively quickly. You sit up higher than you do in a float tube, so it's easier to keep your backcasts off the water behind you. Since only your lower legs are in the water, it's easier to stay warm when floating in cold water. If your pontoon boat has a rear cargo deck, you can even mount an electric motor on it, although I think that if you want to use a motor, you're better off fishing from a larger boat.

Canoes are good all-around watercraft for day trips or extended backcountry travel. They carry a large amount of gear, and the use of paddles makes them very quiet.

Canoes

Of all the styles of boats, canoes are my least favorite to use for fly fishing. They do enable you to reach remote, wilderness areas like the Boundary Waters Canoe Area Wilderness in Minnesota, the Quetico in Ontario, or the Sylvania Wilderness area in Upper Michigan. Extended float trips down remote sections of rivers are also very doable in a canoe.

What I don't like about canoes is that they are very unstable compared to other boats. You have to be careful to keep your weight in the center of the canoe at all times. Also, it is very difficult to fish and maintain your position, unless you're out with a friend. The person in the rear of the canoe should paddle while the person in the bow does the fishing. It's a good option if you work out a system where the two of you switch positions every hour or so. Or find someone who loves paddling, but doesn't like to fish.

The stability of a canoe can be greatly increased with one or two outrigger floats. They can be held out of the water when speed or precise steering is required, but deployed easily when it's time to fish. With outriggers in place, you can even stand up. River Ridge Canoes in Minnesota are designed for fishing. They are relatively stable, and come complete with rod holders and other options (like outrigger floats) that make them ideal for fly anglers.

I was recently on a large lake near my home on a day when the recreational boat traffic made it a little scary for me in my jon boat. While I was doing my best to avoid the huge wakes, here comes a guy in a 12-ft. River Ridge canoe, equipped with outrigger floats, just fishing along like it was no big deal.

Driftboats

Fishing from a driftboat has become synonymous with fly fishing in big western trout streams. Driftboats also work great on larger smallmouth bass

A good driftboat may have a fiberglass, wooden, or aluminum hull. Fiberglass and wooden hulls are quieter and have a lower center of gravity, so they're more stable. A wide hull is more stable and maneuverable than a narrow one.

58

and steelhead rivers in the Midwest.

These boats are designed for fly fishing. They are very maneuverable as well as stable. Many models come with knee braces in the front to help the caster keep his or her balance in rough water. Driftboats will handle rough water with no problem, as long as the person rowing pays attention.

Most fly anglers fish from a driftboat for the first time with an experienced guide on a western river like the Bighorn or the Green. Some popular destinations in the West rent driftboats. Even if you have never rowed one before, it will take you all of two minutes to figure it out.

Motorboats

In recent years, much of my fly fishing has been from motorboats. Any fishing boat will work for fly fishing, but some modifications will make most boats more fly-fisher friendly. Most boats used for freshwater fishing have features that are guaranteed to tangle your flyline, like cleats, electronics, and so on. If you find that you are constantly getting tangled on such things, try covering them with a damp towel.

When fly fishing from a boat, it is critical that you keep the decks and the floor clear of obstacles. If you leave even a pair of pliers on the deck you're casting from, the line will wrap around it every time. Extra rods and reels can be covered with a jacket. If your boat has cleats, a piece of duct tape lengthwise down the cleat will eliminate it as a line grabber.

The worst line grabber of all, though, is your own feet. While fly casting from a boat, it is common to rock back and forth on your feet while casting. When you rock back, the fronts of your feet will lift up slightly. More often than not, your fly-line will go under one of them, and you won't know it until you try to make your presentation— only to have it stopped short by your foot pinning the line to the floor of the boat. I combat this problem by fishing barefoot whenever possible. That way, I can feel if my foot is on the line. You can also try using a stripping basket to contain your loose coils of line, or just keep both feet firmly planted on the floor.

Since most of my fishing is on rivers and small lakes, I have a jon boat that I customized by installing front and back casting decks. A boat like this will handle a wide variety of fly fishing situations. It doesn't draft much water, and is very stable.

Since I got a jon boat, I find that I fish from a float tube less each year. The decks on my boat are relatively free of obstructions. There are some obstructions that are unavoidable, like my electric motor and depth finder, but they are easily "toweled." The best electric motors for fly anglers are ones with a low-profile foot control, such as the Minn Kota Autopilot.

I find that a depth finder is as important when I'm fly fishing as when I'm spin fishing. Even though virtually all fly fishing is done in water 10 ft. deep or less, it's very helpful to know exactly how deep the water is. Some lakes have shorelines that drop off very quickly, even though they may not look like they do. A glance at a depth finder could show that you've been wasting time casting over 30 ft. of water.

I even use a depth finder on my float tube. The Vexilar FL8 is the most user-friendly depth finder currently available. With its flasher design you can see water depth as well as weeds and fish. Vexilar's LPS1 is a handheld model, about the size of a flashlight, that gives a digital reading of the water depth.

Jon boats are a good option in shallow water. Their wide construction makes them very stable and the perfect choice for standing to cast.

CASTING
a Fly

Chapter 7

Flycasting

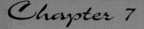

It is the act of fly-casting that really makes fly fishing more enjoyable than other styles of fishing. I never tire of watching my flyline shoot out on a nicely executed cast. While casting a flyline may look almost like a magic trick to a beginner, it really isn't all that difficult, with practice.

There have been hundreds of books and thousands of magazine articles written about the importance of using the right fly. But that really is of little importance if you can't cast the fly to where the fish are.

Becoming a proficient caster requires lots of practice. You should try to practice at least a couple of times per week. Practicing several times per week for ten minutes is usually better than more infrequent, but longer casting sessions.

Flycasting is all about "loading" and "unloading" the rod with the weight of the flyline. Remember that when you are flycasting, you're actually casting the line, and it's carrying the leader and fly with it.

If you have ever cast a spinning or baitcasting rod, you can already make the motions required to cast a fly rod. If you were casting a spinning rod, you would have a lure tied on that was an appropriate weight for the rod. First you would bring the rod back quickly, which causes the weight of the lure to flex or load the rod just as you come forward. You continue to come forward with the rod until it's time to release the line. If you release the line at the right time—just as you cause the rod to unload by stopping the forward part of the cast—your lure will travel straight to its target, pulling the line with it. If you let go too soon, your cast will be a total sky shot. If you let go too late, the lure will splash into the water in front of you.

These same principles apply to flycasting.

I am going to assume that you now have a well-balanced fly-fishing outfit, ideally a 9-ft. fast-action graphite rod, with a reel of an appropriate size and a weight-forward line the same size that the rod is rated for. One tip before we begin: Have a leader on the end of your flyline whenever you're practicing casting. Casting a bare flyline will really beat up the tip of the line.

The following casting instructions are for a right-handed caster.

Practice location

First, you will need to find a good place to practice casting. You should feel comfortable with your flycasting before going fishing. I learned a long time ago that it is virtually impossible to teach someone how to cast on the water with a fly tied on. You need to practice casting in a place where there is no possibility of catching a fish. If you try to learn to cast on the water, the possibility of catching a fish is too much of a distraction for you to concentrate on your flycasting skills.

A large backyard free of obstructions will work great. Otherwise, a park or football field will do. Just try to pick an open spot that has at least 50

ft. in front and 50 ft. behind you, with clean green grass. Do not ever cast on the street or driveway. This will ruin your flyline in a hurry. Also, try to cast in a place with minimal pedestrian traffic. A person flycasting on the grass just seems to invite comments and questions from passersby—like, "Catching any grass carp?!"

String up the rod

Stringing up your fly rod comes next. Start by stripping about 15 ft. of flyline off the reel. Make sure that the line is coming straight off the front of the reel.

Grab the line just above where the leader is attached and double it up. Run it up through all the guides and the tip (but not the hookkeeper), pulling the leader with it. This is much easier and faster than trying to run the line through the guides by using the tip of the leader. Another benefit of doing it this way is that if the line slips out of your hand in the process, the loop will get stuck in the last guide threaded, saving you the trouble of having to re-thread all the guides.

After you have threaded all the guides, double-check to make sure that you didn't miss any.

If you want, you can now tie a small piece of yarn to the end of your leader to simulate a fly. This isn't required, and I find that when I do this for students in a casting class, I spend as much time tying on new pieces of yarn as I do teaching. You decide if it's a help or more bother than it's worth.

Now strip some more line off the reel and pull it out past the tip so that there's about 30 ft. of line out the end of the rod.

Grip the rod with your casting hand, thumb on top. Keep the rod butt in line with your forearm, and your wrist straight.

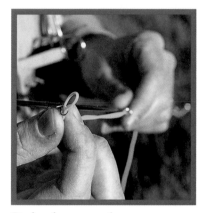

Stringing a rod begins with forming a loop in the flyline, which makes it easier to thread the guides.

Lay your rod down and point it in the direction you'll be casting. If there is a breeze, set up so you are casting into the wind, or with the wind blowing away from your casting side (left to right for a right-handed caster). If it is really windy (over 20 mph), pick a different day.

Walk the end of the line out until it is tight to the reel. Now walk back and pick up the rod with your right hand with your thumb on top of the grip. Strip off another couple of pulls of line so that about 10 ft. of slack line is lying on the grass in front of you. With your left hand, grab the line firmly just ahead of the grip. Place your left hand on your left hip and keep it there. At this point, do not allow any line to slip through your fingers while casting. That will come later. A right-handed caster should have his or her left foot slightly forward while casting.

Backcast

To start, you will need to work on just picking up the line with a backcast, and laying it back down again with a forward cast. You must practice this skill many times before moving on to the next casting level.

Most casting problems seem to be backcast related. There are three things to remember to make a good backcast. Keep them in mind while you are practicing:

1. Apply enough power to the backcast.

2. Stop the rod high (just past vertical).

3. Wait for the line to unroll behind you.

If you do these three things followed by virtually any forward rod movement, you will make a good forward cast.

Even while reading this, you can hold a pencil in your hand and pretend it's a fly rod. Use it to make these casting motions, and you've already begun to "practice" practice casting.

Here are the steps to a good backcast:

• When you apply power to the backcast, most of the power comes from your forearm, not your wrist. Start with the rod pointed straight in front of you. Don't raise the rod above horizontal until you begin to cast.

• To begin the actual backcast, bring the rod straight back smoothly with enough force so that the line will have the momentum to straighten out behind you and load the rod.

If you don't apply enough power, the line will land on the ground behind you before it can load the rod. If you apply too much power, though, you will probably go back too far with the rod tip, which will also cause the line to land on the ground behind you.

Tips for Casting

Practice casting over grass with no trees nearby to interfere with your line. Avoid casting over surfaces such as gravel or asphalt, which can damage your line.

Add some yarn in place of a fly to help you see the end of the leader in the air and on the ground. The yarn won't snag and it is safer than a sharp hook.

The backcast
often causes the most problems for anglers new to fly fishing. Practicing each part of it separately and then putting them all together sometimes helps the learning process.

In my experience of teaching both men and women how to flycast, men try to "kill" it by using too much force, while women often "baby" it.

Be sure to keep your left hand on your left hip with the line gripped tightly in it.

• While applying power to the backcast, your arm speed should accelerate with your wrist locked. Stop the backcast when the rod is just past vertical. Allow your wrist to flex or "open up" as you stop. The line will always travel in the direction the rod is going, so if you bring the rod too far back on the backcast, the rod tip will be pointed at the ground, and the line will hit the ground behind you.

You need to stop the rod high and cleanly. When you stop the backcast, every muscle in your arm should be flexed.

Resist the temptation to raise your casting arm while making your backcast. If the line is hitting the ground behind you, it's probably because you're bringing the rod tip back too far—and raising your arm higher won't stop it. Your casting hand should always be at or below your shoulder height while casting.

• After you have applied enough power to the backcast and stopped the rod high, you now need to wait for the backcast to unroll behind you. This is probably the biggest challenge for novice casters.

Don't be in a hurry. After you stop the backcast, count "one thousand one" before making the forward cast. This will give the line the time it needs to unroll behind you and load the rod. If you come forward before the line has unrolled, you will hear a crack-the-whip sound and your forward cast will barely make it past the end of your rod. So remember to WAIT!

• Making a good backcast is easier if you can get in the habit of watching it right from the beginning. It's easy to ignore what your backcast looks like since it is behind you, but if you watch over your shoulder, you'll be able to see if you're going back too far with the rod, or not waiting long enough.

When you stop your backcast, your line should be pointing straight back off the tip of the rod, parallel to the ground. You will find it easier to watch your backcast if you cast slightly sidearm.

Forward cast

The basic steps to a good forward cast are just as easy to learn:

• Just as your backcast unrolls, begin your forward cast by accelerating smoothly as you bring the rod forward, keeping your wrist locked "open."

• Complete the forward cast by stopping the rod sharply when it's pointing just above the horizon. Flex your wrist forward at the same time. You should still have your left hand on your left hip with the line gripped tightly.

• While making the forward cast, make sure that it is on the same "plane" as the backcast. If you made a sidearm backcast, make sure your forward cast is also sidearm. Think of your forward cast as being almost a mirror image of your backcast.

• If all went well, your flyline should now be unrolled neatly on the ground in front of you. If it is, you are the greatest flycasting student of all time!

Chances are, however, your first cast barely made it past the end of your rod. So start over again.

• If the line came close to lying all the way out in front of you, you can do another cast right away. If the line landed in a heap in front of you, set the rod down and walk the line out again. It is very difficult to make a good backcast if there is a lot of slack in the line to start with.

Get in the habit of pausing for a few seconds between casts. Use this pause to think about how good your cast was, and how you can improve the next one. Too often, I see novice fly casters turn into "casting robots" by quickly picking up and laying down the line many times in a row, not really thinking about what they're doing. If you haven't cast a fly rod before, it can actually become tiring, so pace yourself. If you should develop a blister (which is not that uncommon) put a bandage on it or wear a golf glove.

If your casts are turning out less than perfect, I'll bet a dollar that you're not applying enough power to the backcast, going back too far with the rod, or not waiting for the backcast to unroll. It can help if you have someone else watch you cast. Even if they don't flyfish themselves, they still might be able to see what's going wrong. Another option is to set up a video camera and tape yourself casting from both the side and the front for a few minutes. Then you can see for yourself how your casts look.

The forward cast can also be broken into several steps—each having its own challenges. Put together, you're ready to catch some fish!

False cast

After you have mastered the pick-up and lay-down routine, it's time to learn how to false cast, which accomplishes several things. First, if you were actually fishing, false casting helps to rid a dry fly of excess water. False casting also helps the caster to aim at the target. Finally, combined with some advanced casting techniques (to be covered later), false casting makes it possible to get more line out. Despite what you may have seen in a movie, however, false casting is not meant to simulate insects flying above the surface of the water.

Here are some easy-to-follow steps to learn how to false cast:

• The first thing to do is to make your backcast as usual. Follow with a forward cast, but stop your cast sooner. Just as the line unrolls out in front of you, make another backcast. Once that unrolls, finish by making another forward cast, stopping with the rod pointed just above the horizon.

• Make sure your left hand is still on your left hip with the line gripped tightly in it throughout the process. If you seem to have a problem with keeping your hand there, try putting your hand (with the line still in it) in your left pants pocket. Also be sure to keep your casting hand at or below shoulder height.

• Beginners often do what I call The Statue of Liberty, by casting with their hand higher than

their head. This is a common reaction to trying to keep your line off the ground. But you just can't apply any power to your cast with your hand up that high. It's the same reason a baseball player doesn't throw a ball with his hand higher than his head.

• While false casting, don't ever make more than two or three backcast/forward cast cycles in a row, whether you're practicing or actually fishing. You will just tire faster, and I have noticed that if a caster makes more than a few cycles, the casts get worse and worse. Whether you are trying to cast 20 ft. or 120 ft., you should be able to do it with two or three backcasts. Besides, you'll never catch a fish while your fly is in the air!

The False Cast

After you lift the line off the water as you would on a normal cast, the backcast unrolls behind you, the line forming a small "J." Next, begin the forward cast, but don't let the line settle on the water. Instead, wait until the small "J" forms in the line again and begin another backcast.

Shoot the line

After you've mastered false casting, you can increase your casting distance by shooting the line. To shoot line, you use the weight of the line that you are casting to pull out the extra line that is lying on the ground at your feet on the forward cast.

To do this you must release the line gripped in your left hand at the right time. Just as you complete the forward cast, simply lighten your grip on the line with your left hand. Keep your left hand on your left hip while you do this.

Chances are, on your first few attempts at shooting the line, you will let go too soon. With practice, you should be able to shoot 10 ft. of line with 30 ft. of line out the end of your rod. It is very satisfying to feel the "thunk" when all the line shoots out and pulls tight against the reel.

To gradually increase the amount of line you have out, shoot out a few feet of line on each forward false cast. The ability to do this is very important if you want to cast any distance at all.

Before making another cast, you must strip in the extra line that you just shot out. Keep the rod low and grab the line with your left hand just above the grip. Open up the front two fingers on your right hand and place the line in them. Close your fingers, and strip the line in by grabbing it behind your right hand with your left. Several 2-ft.-long pulls should get the right amount of line back in.

Stripping in line is also how you retrieve the fly or bring in a fish, so it is worth practicing to make sure you get it right.

As your casting skills improve, you can start to false cast with more line out the end of your rod. The more line you can false cast, the more you can shoot out behind it. If you want to be able to cast even farther, you need to add some skills.

In most fly-fishing situations, being able to cast consistently

Stripping in Line

Place the line over the index and/or middle finger of your rod hand. Pinch the line against the rod grip.

Grasp the line with your other hand; pull down while keeping pressure on the line with your rod hand.

and accurately at 20 to 30 ft. is more important than being able to cast long distances. Some fly anglers even say that you never need to cast beyond 30 ft.; but it usually turns out that they themselves can't cast beyond 30 ft.

Sometimes you do have to cast 40, 50, or even 60 ft. to get your fly to the fish. Besides, it's fun to see just how much line you can cast, and the skills needed to cast long distances are the same ones you need to cast short distances when it's windy.

While you're fishing, don't try to cast beyond what your current skills will allow. If you can cast 30 ft. comfortably but can't cast 50, don't try to cast 50. Keep practicing, and work up to it.

In order to be able to cast long distances, you must learn how to haul on the line. Hauling means adding speed and velocity to your cast by making fast pulls on the line with your left hand while casting.

• A single haul is fairly easy to learn if you have mastered false casting. Start out like you normally would, with 30 ft. of line extended in front of you. Pull another 20 ft. of line off the reel and let it lie on the ground at your feet.

Grab the line just ahead of the grip with your left hand. Make your backcast as usual, but strip hard (haul) on the line with your left hand at the same time. You should haul the line to your left hip. This causes the line to move much faster, and the rod to load sooner.

Keep the line in your left hand gripped tightly at your left hip. Stop the backcast and come forward as usual. When you stop the forward cast, release the line in your left hand as before. You should find that you can shoot

Single and Double Haul

A single haul begins when you make a short, smooth downward motion during the acceleration phase of the backcast, stripping hard on the line.

For a double haul, bring your line hand back up immediately after the haul. Then let the line unroll behind you as you would on a normal backcast.

Make the second haul, equal in length to the first, during the acceleration phase of the forward cast.

Finally, release the line from your left hand at the end of the forward cast. Your left hand should still be at your left side.

more line than ever.

• The double haul is the casting technique that is used when maximum distance or casting efficiency is desired. Every other aspect of your fly casting must be at 100% before you attempt to double haul, and it will still take a lot of practice.

You start the double haul the same as a single haul: As your backcast unrolls behind you, take your left hand with the line still gripped tightly in it and feed line into the backcast by moving your left hand in the direction your rod is pointing in.

When the backcast unrolls, begin your forward cast by hauling down on the line across your body, stopping when your left hand is at your left side. Follow this haul closely with your forward cast.

If you timed everything right, your second haul and your forward cast should end simultaneously. Release the line from your left hand at the same time. Your left hand should still be at your left side. If you do it right, you can shoot out about as much line as you want to have stripped off your reel.

Roll cast

The roll cast is one that all fly anglers should know. It is used when obstructions behind you, like bushes or trees, would prevent making a backcast. The cast is actually quite easy to do.

You'll never be able to cast much farther than 30 ft. with a roll cast, but the ability to make any cast at all with zero backcast room is invaluable, especially when stream fishing. You do have to be on the water for this to really work properly.

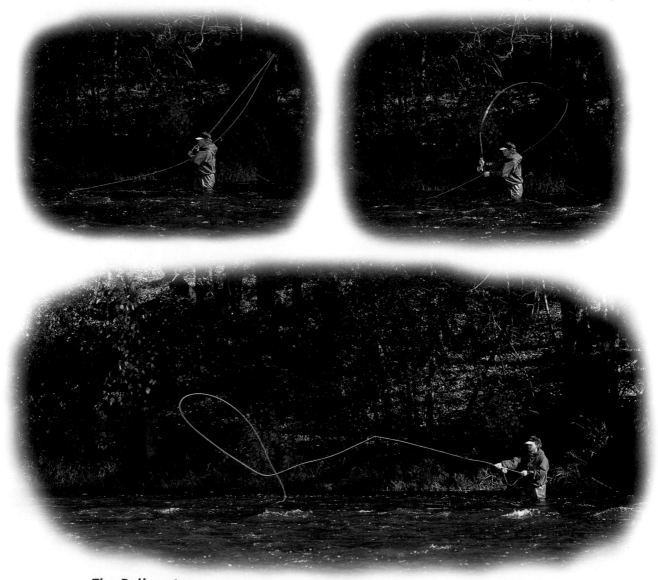

The Roll cast allows you to cast line forward without a backcast, so you can get into tight places where you wouldn't dare risk a backcast.

Start with about 30 ft. of line out the end of your rod. (When roll casting, it is okay for your casting hand to go above shoulder height.) Grab the line just above the grip with your left hand, and place your left hand on your left hip. Now slowly bring the rod back, just past vertical.

I have to emphasize how important it is to bring the rod back slowly. On your first attempts, do it in slow motion. Be sure you wait until the line is hanging straight down off the tip of the rod before proceeding with your roll cast.

Now make the cast by bringing the rod down and forward sharply, accelerating and then stopping with the rod pointing just above the horizon. The line should neatly unroll onto the water in front of you. The biggest problem that beginners have with roll casting is trying to do it too fast.

A final tip

Trying to learn how to flycast from text and photos is difficult—please don't get frustrated and quit because it doesn't seem to be going right. It will be helpful to read over this chapter several times even before trying your first cast; then re-read it after each practice casting session.

You may get additional help from a flycasting video. There are several good ones, and I highly recommend *The Essence of Flycasting* by Mel Krieger.

The best way of all to fine-tune your skills is to get a lesson or two from an experienced flycasting instructor. These people know how to cast and how to teach someone else to do it. Your local fly shop may be able to recommend casting instructors in your area.

Overlining the Rod

Whenever I have a casting student that just isn't getting it, I have a trick that almost always works. "Overlining" the rod makes it load very quickly and easily without much line out.

To overline your rod, temporarily replace your flyline with one that is two sizes bigger than what your rod is rated for. When you make a backcast with this heavy line, you'll really feel the rod load up.

Since this heavy line will be used for practice purposes only, you can get an inexpensive weight-forward type. You will have to cut about 30 ft. of line off the back end (running line end) of this heavy line for it to fit on your reel. Or you may have a friend who already has a heavy line on a reel that you can use to practice.

When I set up a struggling casting student this way, he or she will often say, "Oh, I get it" after the first cast. After a few minutes of casting with the heavy line, casting with the proper-weight flyline comes much easier because now the student knows how a good backcast should look and "feel."

You're probably wondering why you shouldn't use the heavy line all the time. While the heavy line will make your rod easy to cast at short distances, you won't have much delicacy with it. Also, the heavy line will overpower your rod if you try to cast beyond 30 ft.

CATCHING
Fish on Flies

Chapter 8

Where to Fish

Fishing in the right place is the biggest key to your success—far more important than other variables that anglers often agonize over. It doesn't matter what fly you're using if there are no fish in the area. In order to be successful, you have to fish where the fish are.

However, as fly-fishing guru Larry Dahlberg says, that's not always where you want the fish to be. Just because a spot looks good, or because you caught some there two months before, doesn't mean that any fish are there now. Learning the biology of the different fish in your area—such as when and where they spawn and their temperature and habitat needs—will give you a better understanding of why some spots consistently produce.

The first thing to do is to locate a productive body of water for the species you want to catch. Don't try to target a particular species in a body of water where they aren't commonly found. Just because someone tells you he or she caught a pike in a certain lake once doesn't mean that the lake has a high population of pike, or is conducive to fly fishing.

You can start your search for productive lakes and streams at your local fly shop. The staff members usually know the best places in your area to fly fish. If you have no fly shops in your area, a general tackle store or even a bait shop can offer some advice on lakes or streams with good fish populations.

Each state Department of Natural Resources office does lake surveys periodically to study fish populations. Fisheries technicians survey fish populations in a particular lake either by placing nets in the lake, or by electrofishing, and these surveys are public information. These lake surveys can be accessed through the Internet, or by calling your state's fisheries office and requesting them. Be sure that the survey you are looking at is current—less than ten years old—before getting too excited about the information.

Checking with local tackle shops or the DNR will likely give you information to get you headed in the right direction. But you still have to get out there and fish, probably several times, to determine if the lake or stream is any good. Keep in mind that some lakes or streams are more productive at certain times of the year than others. You may already know from firsthand experience with a spinning rod where to find good populations of catchable fish. You will fly fish with much more confidence for the first time in an area where you've already caught fish on spinning tackle.

The following is an overview of where to begin your search for fish on lakes and streams.

Lakes

Lakes can be quite intimidating to an angler armed with a fly rod. No one ever said that fly fishing is a great way to cover water. If you're fishing a particular lake for the first time, there is no shame in using a spinning rod to quickly fish through an area to get a feel for the lake. You may want to start out on smaller lakes, where your location possibilities are narrowed a bit. If you are fishing on a large lake for the first time, try to break the lake down into smaller sections, and just fish one section. You can

try other sections of the lake on future outings.

Concentrations of fish will usually be found in or near some kind of cover. Before fishing an area, ask yourself, "Why would a fish be here?" Fish need cover to hide from larger predators and to ambush prey. Cover comes in many forms, such as weeds, fallen trees, rocks, boat docks, bridge pilings and so on.

Weed cover

In natural lakes with clear water, weeds are usually the most common and most used type of cover. Weeds provide oxygen as well as cover to the

The thick canopy of vegetation at the surface and several feet below it provides shade, security, and cooler temperatures for largemouth bass.

fish. Concentrating your efforts on weed edges is usually the most productive method. Predatory fish will hide just inside the weeds, waiting for prey to come by.

Examples of weed edges commonly fished by fly anglers are lily pads and bullrushes. These plants usually grow in shallow water, and are a favorite of bass and panfish.

On bright sunny days, fish may move deeper into the weed growth. If the edges aren't producing, you may have to go in after them. Be sure to use weedless flies and a very heavy tippet. Some weeds, like cabbage and coontail, grow in deeper water, often covering extensive areas. You can fish the edge of deep weed beds with a fast-sinking line, or cast over the top with a floating or slow-sinking line. Deeper weedbeds are where you are most likely to encounter pike, or even muskies.

Other cover

Locating fish in a lake with minimal or no weed growth is difficult for me. I'm used to fishing in natural lakes that usually have abundant weed growth. Lakes without weeds usually have dark water that prevents weed growth.

If there are no weeds, look for other obvious forms of cover. Man-made reservoirs often lack heavy weed growth. Sometimes these lakes have standing trees in them, leftover from before the area was flooded. Trees in this situation are fish magnets, as are trees that have fallen in along the shoreline.

Some lakes experience heavy algae blooms in the summer, turning the water the color of pea soup. When a lake blooms, many of the weeds die off, forcing the fish to locate other cover. If boat docks are present, they become a favorite form of cover, especially for bass. Casting a noisy popper alongside a dock under these conditions can bring explosive strikes.

Small Streams

I grew up fishing for trout in small streams with worms. My grandfather taught me how to trout fish. We used fly rods and reels with floating flylines and tapered leaders, with a tiny split shot and a small hook baited with a small worm. This rig would be gently roll-cast to the head of a pool or deep run, and would drift naturally to the fish.

My early experiences with worm fishing taught me a lot about how to catch trout on flies later. I learned early on where in a stream the trout were most likely to be found. I also learned that after it rained, trout became easier to catch as the water muddied and food, such as bugs and worms, was washed in.

I caught my first trout on a fly when I was 11. By the time I was a teenager, I greatly preferred the challenge of trying to catch fish on a fly over the relative ease of catching them on a worm.

When I say a small stream, I mean streams that range in width from about 10 ft. to about 100 ft. Small streams are best fished by wading, although a canoe or pontoon boat can be used to float into otherwise inaccessible areas.

The way you approach a spot that you plan to fish on a small stream is very important. Whenever possible, approach a spot from downstream. Fish in streams will always be facing into the current, so it is relatively easy to get close to them if you come up from below them. Sometimes it may be necessary to keep a low profile, for example by crouching down or even kneeling. If a trout spots you, and recognizes you as a potential source of danger, your chances of catching it are reduced to about zero.

Small streams (as well as some larger streams) can be divided into four different water types: riffles, runs, pools, and flats.

Riffles

Riffles are defined as areas with fast current, broken on the surface with a rocky bottom. Riffles are formed where a stream flows downhill faster than elsewhere. They are well oxygenated, and usually have high concentrations of nymphs and other food items.

Riffles are where the most active, or catchable, fish will be found. Fish hang out in riffles for one reason: to eat! Even large fish will feed actively in riffles only a foot deep. They know that with the broken surface of the water they are hard to see.

Since the current in a riffle is moving fairly fast, the fish holding there don't have a lot of time to inspect your fly before it is swept downstream, so your fly pattern is less critical than in other water types.

All four water types are often found within a short distance on a stream. The shallow water and fast current of a riffle (1) deepens and slows to form a run (2). As the water slows even more, a pool (3) is formed. As the water speeds up again it flows into a flat (4).

The broken surface will also hide any errant casts.

Runs

When a riffle starts to slow down, the water usually deepens, forming a run. In a run, the surface of the water starts to smooth out, but there is still good current.

A deep run located above a pool is where I usually start fishing. When fish in the pool decide to start feeding, they move up into the run. A run has enough depth for the fish to be comfortable, and enough current to get a good drift with your fly.

Be sure to thoroughly fish a run before moving to the riffle above it. You don't want to miss any opportunities for fish.

Pools

Eventually, the current will slow even more and the water will become even deeper, forming a pool. These areas are where the deepest water in a stream is found.

A pool often holds large numbers of fish, and the largest fish in a given area will usually be found in or near a deep pool. On trout streams, it is possible to look into a deep pool on a sunny day and see dozens of trout lying on the bottom.

Fish sitting in a deep pool are usually inactive, and not likely to take anything other than a worm dangled in their face. I suggest you leave the pools for the bait fishermen.

Flats

At the lower end of a pool, the water becomes more shallow, and the current speed picks up again. This type of area is called a flat. Eventually the flat ends and another riffle starts.

To determine where on a small stream you'll be most likely to catch fish, remember to fish where the fish are. Or better yet, fish where the catchable fish are.

On a small trout stream, for example, you're likely to see fish all over the place. Flats may look inviting: You can often see fish in the shallow water, and you may even see them rising, eating insects off the surface.

The problem with trying to catch fish on flats is that the surface of the water is very flat, and the water shallow. That means the fish will be very spooky, and one mistake, such as a bad cast, will send the fish to deeper water.

It isn't impossible to catch fish in spots like this, especially during a big hatch on overcast days or when the water is slightly murky, but I recommend that you spend your time fishing for easier fish.

Large Streams

During the summer months, most of my fishing is on large streams like the Mississippi or St Croix rivers. I enjoy the lack of crowds almost as much as I enjoy the great fishing. Large streams like these are best fished from some type of boat, although wading can be an option if the water is low.

Water levels are the most important variable determining fish location and activity level. Many anglers prefer low water because the lower level concentrates the fish in the remaining deep water.

If you plan on wading, you will want the water to be at a low level, as wading a large stream when the water is high is difficult, if not dangerous.

Since most of my fishing on large streams is from a boat, I'll take normal-to-high water anytime for several reasons. Normal-to-high water makes navigation easier, cutting down on ruined props. It also seems to make the fish more active, and forces fish to move to shoreline areas, where they can escape most of the force of the strong current. Under these conditions, it is easy to tell where they're going to be.

The most important thing you need to look for on a large stream with fast-moving water" is "current breaks." This is especially true during normal-to-high water conditions. Current breaks are anything that disrupts the flow of the current, such as points, rocks, or fallen trees. Fish will hold downstream of these obstructions, usually on or near the current "seam," where the fast

current meets the slow water formed by the obstruction. Here, the fish can hold in relatively slow water, waiting for the faster, main current to bring them food.

I have found that in low-water periods, while concentrations of fish can be found in deep holes, the main current speed is slow enough to allow fish to hold virtually anywhere in the river, which makes pinpointing their location difficult. During low-water periods, the overall activity level of the fish is often very low.

While large streams can be harder to read than small streams, you can still predict where active fish are most likely

to be located. The water on large streams is usually less defined than in small streams. While the riffle-run-pool-flat principle still applies, it may be harder to recognize different water types in a large stream.

Many rivers have sections, sometimes long ones, with a relatively slow current from bank to bank. This is especially apparent during low-water conditions. While obvious cover and current breaks still hold fish in slow-current areas, the fish may often be scattered along seemingly featureless banks. In sections like this, one side of the river is usually a little deeper and a little faster than the other side. Most fish will be found on the deeper side, usually located on the outside bend of the river.

If you're in a boat, it's easy to cast to miles of shoreline in a day. Always be looking ahead for where you want your next cast to go.

When bankshooting like this, there is the temptation to always cast the fly right next to the shore. But you shouldn't bother trying to land your fly an inch from the bank if the water is only an inch deep there.

When you see a good current break coming up, like a downed tree, don't cast upstream of it. While active fish will sometimes hold upstream of a current break, it's best to save your cast for the slack water found on the downstream side.

What I like best about fishing streams of all sizes is that once you learn how to locate fish on one stream, it's easy to locate fish on a different stream. No matter what stream or river you're fishing on, a downed tree or rocky point will very likely have fish located downstream of it.

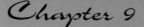

Chapter 9

Panfish

nyone who aspires to be a successful fly angler should start out by targeting panfish. No fish is easier to catch, and after catching a bunch of panfish on a fly, you will have the confidence and skill it takes to go after more difficult fish like bass or trout. Just think of how much fun you'll have in the learning process!

Depending on where you live, panfish can mean sunfish, bluegills, pumpkinseeds, shell-crackers, bream, crappies, and many others. Panfish are the perfect fish for a beginning fly angler. They are common in lakes and rivers throughout the United States. So wherever you live, there is probably a lake nearby with a good population of panfish, and there is no better way to catch them than with a fly rod.

If you live in the South, fly fishing for panfish can be a year-round activity. If you live in a northern state, as I do, the earliest you can start fishing in lakes is probably around mid-April. Soon after the ice goes out, bluegills and crappies move into shallow bays, looking for warm water. Warm water is relative. In early spring, 50°F is warm, and you aren't likely to have good action until the water temp is at least in the 50s. Several warm and sunny days in a row will almost always get the water temp up, and the fish's activity level will go up too.

Setup

For tackle, I prefer a 9-ft., 5- or 6-weight fly rod matched with a weight-forward floating line. Your leader should be between 7 ft. and 9 ft. long, tapered to 3x. Lighter rods like a 3- or 4-weight can also be used, but a slightly heavier rod will enable you to cast farther, especially if it's windy.

If the panfish in your lake run large, the added muscle of the heavier rod will help keep the fish out of the weeds. On a recent bluegill outing, I lost several big fish that I couldn't keep out of the weeds with a 6-weight.

By the way, with a 5- or 6-weight, you are also able to cast smaller bass flies if the opportunity for catching some bass should arise.

Flies

As far as flies go, I can't imagine any small fly that won't catch sunfish and crappies. However, don't make the mistake of using flies that are too small. With a small, size 16 nymph, you will catch plenty of panfish, especially bluegills and pumpkinseeds.

One problem with using flies that are too small is that the fish is often hooked very deeply,

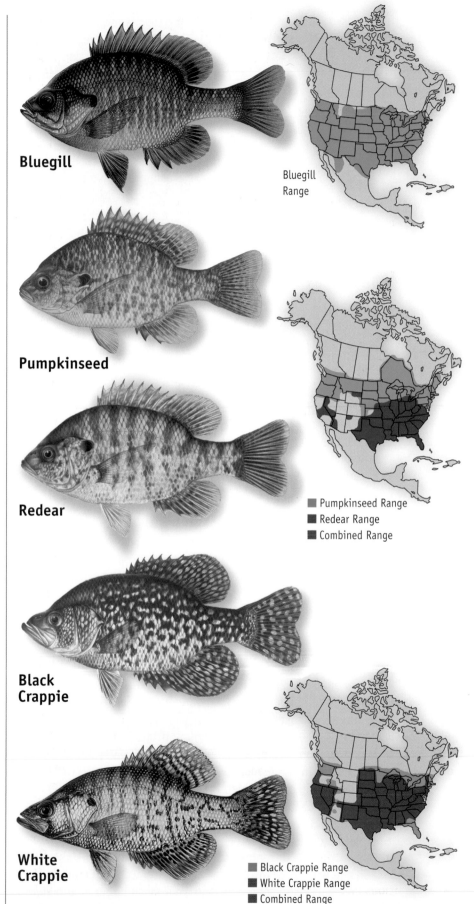

Bluegill

Bluegill Range

Pumpkinseed

■ Pumpkinseed Range
■ Redear Range
■ Combined Range

Redear

Black Crappie

White Crappie

■ Black Crappie Range
■ White Crappie Range
■ Combined Range

size 16 pheasant tail nymph
(actual size)

size 10 wooly worm
(actual size)

size 6 wooly worm
(actual size)

making removing the fly difficult. Using very small flies also encourages 3-in.-long sunfish to take your fly. Even if you haven't caught many fish on a fly before, I know that you can do better than a 3-incher!

Using a more appropriate fly, like a size 10 wooly worm or dragonfly nymph, discourages the really small fish from biting and encourages strikes from larger panfish. If the waters you fish have really big panfish, you may want to go to a size 8, or even a 6. (A fly like one of these is also large enough to be interesting to a passing bass or pike.)

You'll have the most success using subsurface nymphs, but most panfish anglers look forward to the time later in the spring when the sunfish eagerly take poppers, foam spiders, or dry flies off the surface. Surface flies work best for panfish when the water temps are in the 60s or higher, and when the wind is calm.

I remember fly fishing for sunnies when I was a kid. My grandpa would start me out with a new black gnat he had tied himself. At the lakes we fished for sunnies in those days, it was never long before we started catching them.

I noticed that after about ten fish, the fly started to look ragged. After twenty, things were coming unraveled. After thirty fish, the fly was unrecognizable as a black gnat, but the fish loved it more than ever. I wondered why I should start out with a "perfect" fly when it was obvious to me that the more beat up a fly was, the more the fish seemed to like it.

Today, I don't think that it was the appearance of the fly that made the fish like it more, but the fact that the more fish I had caught on it, the more confidence I had in it. The more confidence I had in the fly, the more attention I paid to what I was doing, so the more fish I caught. I also think that as I caught more fish on a particular fly, it began to get a fishy smell on it, adding much to the fly's appeal.

As far as colors go, I usually start with black or olive, and I don't often find the need to change. In some bodies of water, fluorescent colors like chartreuse can also be effective. If you are unsuccessful in catching panfish on a fly, it is very unlikely because of the fly. If you aren't having any luck, try a different area, or wait for the water to warm up.

Many flies that catch sunfish also work great for crappies, especially in the larger sizes. If you are trying to target crappies, though, you should include some minnow-imitating streamer patterns. Crappies have a much larger mouth than other panfish, and while they

A streamer
like this Mickey Finn is a good fly for crappies.

do eat small nymphs, larger flies are usually more effective. Bucktail streamers, like a Mickey Finn or black-nosed Dace, are readily available patterns that are very effective.

Using poppers can also be a lot of fun for crappies. For some reason, when crappies take a surface fly they often come out of the water first and then come down on the fly. Be sure to wait until the fish has the fly before you set the hook.

Barbless hooks

No matter which type of panfish you are after, I highly recommend pinching down the barbs on the hooks of your flies. Fishing with a barbless hook has lots of advantages.

Obviously, the fly comes out of the fish much easier, whether you are keeping the fish or not. A barbless fly will also come out of you much easier, if an errant cast causes you to be wearing a fly where you didn't want one.

Your flies will actually last longer if you pinch down the barbs, because you won't destroy them while trying to extract them from the fish; they just pop right out of the fish's mouth. I guess it is possible to lose a fish because of a barbless fly, but as long as you keep the line tight, losing a fish is unlikely. On many occasions, I have intentionally given a hooked fish some slack line to see if it could rid itself of a barbless fly, and it rarely does.

Blind casting

During the pre-spawn period, you will be doing a lot of blind casting, which means that you can't see the fish, so you must cover the water by making as many casts as you can. Pay special attention to any forms of cover, such as downed trees or weedbeds.

After you have made a cast, lower your rod to the water's surface. If you are using a subsurface fly, begin your retrieve by stripping in line in 6-in. pulls. A surface fly should be fished slowly. Let it sit for a few seconds, then move it with a short, 3-in. strip. After waiting another few seconds, repeat.

Set the hook

One of my top ten rules in all types of fishing is: When in doubt, set the hook! Here are some tips for setting the hook:

• If you are using a surface fly like a popper, you will see the fly disappear in a swirl when a fish eats it. Set the hook by simply lifting up sharply with your rod tip, and stripping line with your line hand at the same time. If you are using a subsurface fly, your line will simply tighten when a fish has the fly.

• When you're fishing for panfish, the hook set doesn't have to be super hard, as might be required if you were bass fishing. But you do need to get the hook stuck into the fish's mouth. If it turns out not to be a fish, or if you are too late on the hook set, your line, leader, and fly will go back over your shoulder, forming a backcast. When the backcast unrolls, make a forward cast as you usually do, and your fly should go right back into the fish zone.

Flies That Will Catch All Kinds of Panfish

These flies are my favorite choices. Many other flies will also work, but you can't go wrong with these.

Dragonfly/ damselfly nymphs, olive, size 6-12.

Damselfly Nymph

Wooly worms, black, brown, olive, or yellow, size 6-12.

Black Wooly Worm

Hare's-ear nymph, size 8-12.

Gold Ribbed Hare's-ear Nymph

Cork or foam poppers, black, white, or yellow, size 8-12.

Yellow Popper

Foam spider, black, white, or yellow, size 8-12.

Foam Spider

Beadhead marabou leech, black or olive, size 8-12.

Beadhead Leech

• Be glad you are using a fly rod: If you were bait fishing with a bobber, you would have to waste valuable fishing time re-baiting after each miss.

• If, on the hook set, you connect with a fish, the rod will be bent, and you should bring the fish in by stripping in line. It can be tricky at first to get the flyline from your line hand into your rod hand. But after a few fish, it will come naturally.

Move your rod hand across your body, and grab the line with the front two fingers on your rod hand. Then bring the fish in by stripping in the line in long pulls. Remember to keep the rod bent. A bent rod means the line is tight, and it is almost impossible to lose a securely hooked fish as long as you keep the line tight.

• Continue to strip in line until you have about a rod's length of line out. If the fish is small, you can swing the fish right up to you. If the fish is a larger one, keep it in the water with the rod still bent until you can grab it. On really large panfish, especially crappies, which have a soft mouth, you may want to use a landing net.

Pre-spawn Locations

I do most of my fly fishing for panfish during the first month or two of open water. There are always good numbers of them in shallow water from ice out, usually mid-April, until after the spawn, in mid-June.

When water temps reach the 50s, panfish begin actively feeding in the shallows, getting ready for the spawn. Although sunfish and crappies try to eat anything they think they can fit in their mouth, most of their food comes as aquatic insects and small minnows, easily imitated by anglers.

Begin your search for pre-spawn sunfish in shallow bays. This is where the warmest water and greatest numbers of active fish are found in the spring. Man-made canals and ditches are also early-spring fish magnets. I know of a canal that is attached to a large lake that absolutely loads up with panfish in the early spring. The canal is several hundred yards long, and about 4-ft. deep. I have caught fish there even when the main lake still had ice on it.

Spawn & Post-spawn Locations

Later in the spring, panfish will begin spawning. Sunfish and crappies usually spawn in water between 1 ft. and 5 ft. deep with a firm bottom. With polarized sunglasses, it is easy to see their spawning beds. They will appear as saucer- to dinner-plate-sized circles on the lake bottom. A popper or foam spider plopped onto or near a spawning bed will almost always draw a strike.

After the spawn, most panfish, especially the larger ones, move into deeper water, where catching them on a fly rod becomes more difficult. While it is possible to catch these deeper panfish on a fly, you're best off trying to catch the panfish that stay shallow.

In the summer, working the edges of weed beds, especially emergent weeds like lily pads and bullrushes, always produces panfish, especially bluegills.

Make a Meal

Panfish got their name for a reason: They often end up in a fry pan. There is absolutely nothing wrong with keeping enough fish for a meal now and then; I enjoy a meal of pan-fried bluegills as much as anyone. Filling your freezer with fillets, however, is another matter. For most of the last century, a successful day of fishing meant catching (and keeping) your limit of fish, even for several days in a row.

The days of filling your freezer with fillets are, or at least should be, long gone. There are many more anglers on the water today than there were fifty years ago, but the number of fish in the water has stayed the same. Panfish have no problem reproducing effectively even in heavily fished waters, but continual harvests of coolers full of large panfish have turned many lakes into small-fish factories.

The only way that this can change is if anglers change their attitudes toward keeping fish. Only take home enough for a good meal for your family.

If you plan on keeping some fish, be sure to have a cooler of ice for keeping your catch in good condition until you clean them. If you fish from a boat, putting them in a live well works great. And if the first couple of fish in the live well don't get any company, you can always release them.

Chapter 10

Trout

J ust mention fly fishing to anyone, and images of an angler standing in a mountain stream casting for trout will almost always come to his or her mind. About ten years ago, the very popular film *A River Runs Through It* came to movie theaters, and interest in fly fishing exploded, especially fly fishing for stream trout.

The film was based on an autobiographical novella by Norman Maclean about his somewhat dysfunctional family living in Montana in the early 1900s. Despite all of their problems, fly fishing was a common bond that held them together.

But these couple of sentences do not come close to doing the story justice. If you haven't seen the movie or read the book, I highly recommend you do. After all, seeing Robert Redford and Brad Pitt pretending to catch trout was inspiration for thousands of new anglers to try their hand at fly fishing. Fly shops across the country experienced a boom in sales, and new fly shops popped up all over the place.

For a variety of reasons, fly

fishing for trout is more difficult than for bass or panfish. Even if your main reason for taking up fly fishing is to fish for trout in streams, I highly recommend that if it is at all possible you try your hand at panfish or bass before venturing out on a trout stream.

Don't let me give you the impression that catching stream trout on flies is so difficult that success on your first outing is impossible—it's not. But then, no one ever said that you have to catch fish to have an enjoyable time on the stream.

There is no way to describe in words what a wonderful place a trout stream is to spend time. The sights, sounds, and smells you experience on a trout stream are worth the trip alone, and actually catching a few trout could be considered a bonus.

Trout Streams

To catch trout with regularity, you should know about the fish first. One of many things that make trout different from other fish species is their need for cool, clean water. Trout are native only to areas that naturally have cold-water streams. Streams that are fed by springs or snowmelt are where trout were originally found in the United States. Huge dams built across warm-water rivers have created cold-water trout fisheries where none historically existed. The water coming out from the bottom of a 100-ft.-deep reservoir is very cold, and has created world-class fisheries in places as unlikely as Arizona.

Trout streams can be grouped into three categories: spring creeks, freestone streams, and tailwater streams. This categorization is rough, however, because many streams will exhibit characteristics of more than one type of stream. For instance, some freestone streams are fed by springs, and some tailwater streams have a spring creek "feel" to them.

Spring creeks

These streams are fed by natural cold-water aquifers. They flow at a fairly constant temperature all year. They are mainly found in the northeastern, midwestern, and western states.

Because of their stable water temperatures, spring creeks provide excellent trout habitat; they don't freeze in any but the very coldest weather, and even during summer hot spells they stay relatively cool.

Spring creeks usually have abundant weed growth, which holds aquatic insect life—a must for good trout populations.

Spring creeks generally have slow to moderate current and very clear water. They often produce numbers of surprisingly large trout.

Freestone streams have moderate to fast currents with numerous riffles, pools, and runs. The best of them are spring-fed for ideal water temperature.

Tailwater streams sometimes have stable water flow, allowing development of rooted vegetation that holds many aquatic insects.

Freestone streams

Fed mainly by runoff from rain or snowmelt, most freestone streams are found in or near mountainous regions, but there are some throughout the northern United States.

In order for a freestone stream to support trout, there must be enough flow to keep the stream from freezing solid in the winter, and it must stay cool enough in the summer to keep the trout from dying. Trout thrive in water that is between 40°F and 60°F, but will die if the water temps stay in the 70s for very long.

Tailwater streams

These streams are formed on the downstream side of dams that create huge, deep reservoirs. They are found all over the United States, mostly in the West. Some of the best are in the South and Southwest.

When a large dam creates a reservoir that may be hundreds of feet deep, the water flowing out of the bottom is very cold. Some of the best tailwater trout streams are ones that had no population of trout whatsoever before the dam was in place.

Trout Species

North America is home to four types of stream trout. Actually, there are more than four if you include some rare and very local species, or if you include the many subspecies or different races of some kinds of trout. For the purposes of this book, though, there are four kinds: brook, rainbow, cutthroat, and brown.

While each species has its own preferences for food and habitat, they all are really quite similar. It isn't uncommon in some streams to catch two or more different kinds of trout out of the same spot on the same fly.

Brook trout

Technically, this native fish belongs to the char family along with arctic char and lake trout. Brook trout, or "brookies" as most trout anglers call them, were originally found only in the eastern and midwestern states, as well as eastern Canada. They have now been transplanted to many suitable streams in the West.

In most places, brookies are small fish. On the spring creeks that I fish, a 10-inch is a big one, and I don't think I've ever caught one over a foot long. There aren't many places in the United States you could expect to catch them much bigger with any regularity. Some Canadian rivers have populations of brook trout that regularly grow to over 20 in. long.

The fact that they're usually so small doesn't seem to diminish their popularity with trout anglers. They are arguably the most beautiful freshwater fish, and no photograph can do them justice. Since brookies can live only in the coldest and purest water, the places you find them are invariably as beautiful as the fish—usually tiny spring creeks or mountain brooks.

Brookies' willingness to take a fly is another quality that makes them popular. It has actually made them too popular; fishing pressure has hurt many brook trout populations. But fishing pressure alone has not done nearly as much damage to them as loss of habitat has. A combination of poor farming practices and urban sprawl has wiped out brookies in much of their original range.

Brookies spawn in the fall, and it is when they are in their spawning colors that they have the most striking appearance. The males become the most brilliantly colored, with scarlet sides, white-edged fins, and a dark green back broken up with vermiculated markings and bright spots.

Brookies, like most trout, feed mainly on insects, but also eat a lot of minnows.

Rainbow trout

This species is native only to West Coast streams that flow to the Pacific Ocean. Because rainbow trout can adapt to a wide variety of habitats, they have been widely transplanted. Populations of rainbows are now found in almost every state, even Hawaii, providing many trout-fishing opportunities.

Rainbows can be found in all types of trout streams. They can grow to very large sizes. In some western streams, they regularly grow to over 20 in., and sometimes quite a bit larger. Rainbow trout are well known

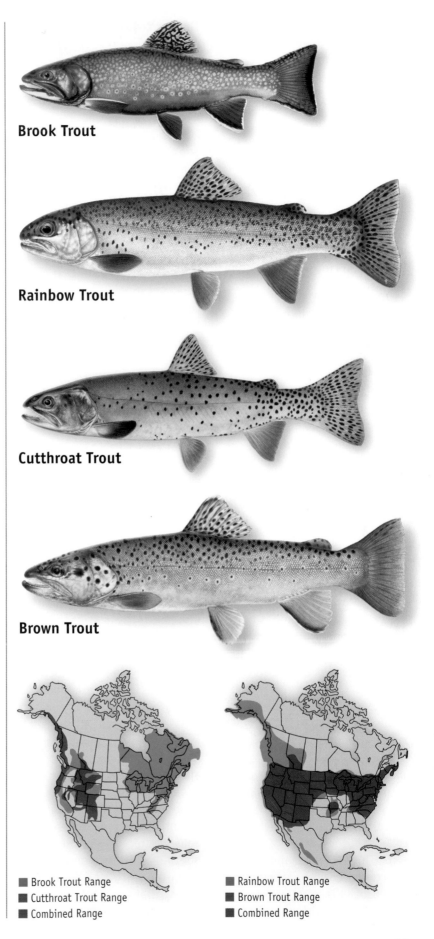

Brook Trout

Rainbow Trout

Cutthroat Trout

Brown Trout

■ Brook Trout Range
■ Cutthroat Trout Range
■ Combined Range

■ Rainbow Trout Range
■ Brown Trout Range
■ Combined Range

for their spirited fight when hooked, often jumping and making fast runs.

Rainbows can vary greatly in color from fish to fish. They generally have silvery flanks with a grayish or greenish back, and the red or pink stripe down their sides gives them their name. As spawning time approaches in the spring, their coloration often becomes darker and more vivid.

Rainbow trout feed on a wide variety of foods, but eat mostly insects and crustaceans. They are also very fond of fish eggs, and can often be found holding downstream of spawning salmon or other trout, gobbling up stray eggs.

Cutthroat trout

This trout is native to the Rocky Mountains and West Coast. Cutthroats have an appearance similar to rainbows, but red slash marks located in the throat area, along with fewer spots, set them apart.

Cutthroats are much more sensitive to water quality than rainbows. As a result, they are found almost exclusively in their native waters. Perhaps the best-known cutthroat fishing is found in Yellowstone Park, but good populations can also be found in remote locations in other areas of the West. In many areas, cutthroats are slowly disappearing, as they are being replaced by rainbow or brook trout.

Like rainbows, cutthroats spawn in the spring. In streams with both cutthroat and rainbow trout, the two may interbreed, which creates a hybrid called a cutbow.

Cutthroats feed mainly on insects and small crustaceans, and they usually take any reasonable imitation with enthusiasm.

Brown trout

This species is not native to North America. It was brought here from Europe in the late 1800s, at about the same time carp were introduced. Brown trout were scorned by trout anglers at first. People viewed them as ugly, cannibalistic fish that were too difficult to catch. But two things have made them the most popular trout species in America, even though they aren't a native trout: their ability to thrive in waters that had degraded to the point where they would no longer support the beloved brook trout, and the fact that they can grow to large sizes.

Browns often do seem more difficult to catch than other trout, but for most folks, this makes them that much more appealing.

I don't know how anyone ever considered a brown trout to be an ugly fish. While they don't have the striking appearance of a brook or rainbow trout, their golden sides, black spots, and dark-brown back make them a fish worthy of a photo.

Browns can be found in many different types of streams across the country. In most streams, the average size is 10 in. to 14 in., but they can grow much larger in streams with good habitat and food.

Like other trout, they feed mainly on insects, but once brown trout get to be over about 16 in. long, they start to feed less on insects and more on larger food items like minnows and crayfish. Someone recently showed me a photo of a 17-in. brown next to an unidentified 6-in.-long rodent that was in its stomach. I also remember my grandpa cleaning a 16-in. brown that had recently eaten a 5-in. trout.

Setup

Depending on the stream, the method you'll be using and your own personal preferences, you can use a rod as light as a 3-weight and as heavy as a 7-weight for stream-trout fishing. A 5-weight rod, 8 to 9 ft. long, will work in a wide variety of stream-trout-fishing situations. A 3-weight, or an even lighter rod, has its place on small streams where short casts with small flies is typical.

Go fishing on a windy day, though, and you'll be wishing you had a slightly heavier rod. A 6-, or even a 7-weight is very useful on larger streams or when using big flies.

Run into a good hatch when using a heavier rod, and you'll be wishing for the delicacy a lighter rod provides.

I always have 4-, 5-, and 6-weights with me when I head to a trout stream. That way, I know I'm covered no matter what happens. But since you're just getting started, I recommend a 5-weight as an all-around choice.

Be sure that your reel is the right size for your rod, and have a weight-forward floating line spooled onto it. You should always be prepared with an assortment of tapered leaders and spools of tippet material. Leaders 7$1/2$ to 9 ft., tapered to between 3x and 6x, and spools of tippet 3x to 6x should always be in your vest. Refer to the tippet rating/fly size chart on page 21 to determine what size tippet you should be using.

Down-and-across fishing with a subsurface fly, like a gold-ribbed hare's-ear nymph is a great way for an angler to cover water, searching for active fish.

Gold-ribbed Hare's-Ear Nymph

Down-and-across Fishing

The easiest way for a beginner to catch stream trout on flies is to use a "down-and-across" presentation with a subsurface fly. Down-and-across fishing is a great way for an angler to cover water, searching for active fish. Actively feeding fish are the easiest ones to catch.

This method works best in riffles and runs on streams, or sections of streams, that are at least 50 ft. across. Approach a likely-looking location from above, and begin fishing at the top of the riffle. You may want to keep a low profile, and move slowly to avoid alarming the fish.

My grandpa taught me a long time ago to catch the close ones before moving on to try for fish on the other side of the stream. So start out by making a couple of short casts from the bank. You should cast straight across or slightly down the stream, and allow the fly to swing across the current until it is below you.

After making your first couple of short casts, make a couple of longer ones, and then step into the stream. Gradually work your way downstream, one cast at a time. Make a cast, let it swing across the current until it is below you, take a step downstream and repeat.

You should keep moving, looking for active fish. As the fly is swinging in the current, try to imagine exactly where it is at all times, and follow its path with your rod tip.

You can give the fly extra action by stripping in line in short pulls, or twitching the rod tip. The line should be fairly tight during the process, and a strike from even a small trout will feel like quite a jolt. You don't need to make much of a hook set to connect with the fish; just tighten up by lifting the rod tip.

You're probably wondering by now why I haven't mentioned what fly you should use. I could certainly list several specific fly patterns that mimic various life stages of different insects, but in this style of fishing, you are searching for actively feeding fish, and as long as you use a reasonable fly and cover water, you will get strikes. So what's reasonable? It depends somewhat on the stream, water clarity, and other factors; but if you tie on a good old hare's-ear nymph, and

swing it through riffles and runs the way I've described, you will catch fish. You could substitute a pheasant-tail nymph, caddis pupa, soft hackle, or any other small, buggy-looking fly and have the same success.

Some might say that fishing this way mimics the way an emerging mayfly or caddisfly behaves as it swims toward the surface. This may be true, but I think that it works because you cover so much water that you contact many active fish in the process and, therefore, get many strikes. I sometimes think that the real reason this method works is because of the unnatural movement of your fly across the current. This unnatural movement attracts more attention from active fish. Whatever the reason, it works. Remember—cover lots of water.

The down-and-across style of fishing also lends itself well to using streamers. Streamers generally represent minnows or other large food items.

Down-and-across fishing is an easy way for beginners and experienced anglers alike to catch trout. Make a cast, let it swing, take a step down, and repeat. On some days, it seems as if you get a good yank every few minutes.

Fishing with Nymphs

On some days, strikes on a swinging fly can be few and far between. Nymph fishing is the most consistent way to catch trout under most circumstances. While somewhat more complicated than down-and-across fishing, it's not difficult to master. Once you learn how to nymph fish, you'll be able to catch trout in any stream, any time.

Nymph fishing involves using a weighted imitation of a mayfly or stonefly nymph, a caddisfly or midge larva, or a crustacean, drifted naturally along the stream bottom. Nymph fishing is most productive in fast-moving stream sections, like riffles and runs.

To determine what fly would be the best choice, spend a few minutes turning over rocks and finding out what kind of nymphs are the most prevalent. You don't have to have exact imitations, but having a nymph tied on that is the approximate size, shape, and color of the nymphs in your stream will ensure that you fish with confidence.

I use nymphs almost exclusively in areas with medium-to-fast current. Imagine you are a trout, finning in the riffle, waiting for food. Now imagine how fast any drifting nymphs are actually traveling by your head. Do you really think that a trout has time to decide exactly what color a nymph is supposed to be as it drifts by? If trout had vision that good, we'd never catch them.

Flies

Two of the most popular flies used today in nymph-style fishing are the orange scud and the prince nymph. These two flies account for thousands of trout every year, but they don't really look like any nymphs found naturally in trout streams.

Lift a rock, then check for nymphs or larvae on the underside. This is a good way to collect caddis cases, stonefly nymphs, and other insect larvae.

• Orange scuds work because orange is usually visible underwater, not because they match the color of natural scuds. Natural scuds are always the color of the stream bottom, usually tan or grayish olive.

Orange Scud

• A prince nymph is supposed to represent a stonefly. This fly works because the white wings contrast against the fly's dark body. Depending on the lighting and water clarity, either the dark body or the white wings will be visible to the trout.

Prince Nymph

Strike indicators

There are many ways to rig your leader for nymph fishing. Most nymph fishing setups use one or more of the following: a weighted fly, split shot or other additional weight, and a strike indicator. There are many ways to put these components together, and it seems that everybody has a favorite way.

Strike indicators have become synonymous with nymph fishing. Depending on how you rig up, a strike indicator can be just that—a strike indicator—or it can work much like a spin angler's bobber. You will catch more fish while nymphing if you use strike indicators.

If you're going to use an indicator, make sure that it is one you can see. Strike indicators are available in many colors, usually bright fluorescents like orange, pink, or chartreuse. I have found that pink shows up the best under most conditions,

but depending on the lighting, other colors can be a better choice. For instance, when the sun is low and directly in front of you, the glare off the water can make it impossible to see any indicator other than a dark-colored one. I always have one or two black indicators in my vest for such times. If you can't find any dark ones, color a bright one with a marker.

There are many different styles of strike indicators available. You should try out at least a few different styles to determine which work best for you.

• Foam pinch-on indicators were one of the first widely available strike indicators. To use one, peel it off the sheet and pinch it in place on your leader. They are cheap, but once one's in place, you can't move it, and they're difficult to remove.

• Roll-on indicators are made of the same material as pinch-ons. They have the advantage of being easy to cast, but they aren't very buoyant and are difficult to see. I would use this style of indicator only on small streams, or for making short casts.

• Strike putty is a moldable strike indicator material. I use strike putty a lot because it makes it easy to vary the size of your indicator. I use Loon's Bio-strike, which is reusable and biodegradable. If you don't anchor it in place on your leader properly, it will eventually start to slide, or come off altogether. I don't

have a problem with it coming loose because I always anchor it on a knot high up on the leader, near the flyline. Be sure to wet your fingers before using the putty, and if it is a cold day, keep it warm by storing it in a shirt pocket next to your body. Strike putty becomes rock hard and unusable when it gets cold.

• Yarn indicators might be the most popular style of indicator in use today. People like them because they don't seem as much like a bobber as other styles of indicators. After all, they're made of yarn, not foam or cork. For them to work properly, they do have to be fairly large.

Because they aren't as buoyant as foam or cork indicators, yarn indicators work best in areas that aren't too turbulent. One widely available yarn indicator is the Tip-Off brand.

To ensure maximum buoyancy, treat your yarn indicators with fly floatant before using.

• Skip's Turn-on Indicators are a clever design. They are made of two different-colored pieces of foam held together with an elastic band. To use one, lay your leader in the slit, pull the two pieces of foam apart and twist them in opposite directions. They are easy to move on your leader, or to remove altogether.

• Corkies are manufactured by the Yakima Company to be used as a steelhead

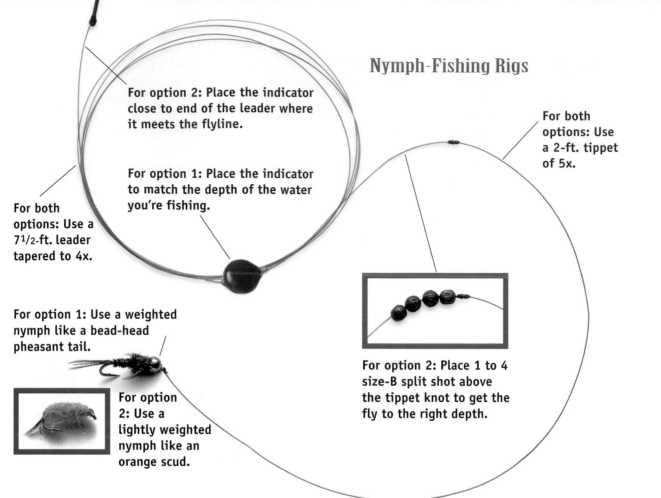

For option 2: Place the indicator close to end of the leader where it meets the flyline.

For option 1: Place the indicator to match the depth of the water you're fishing.

For both options: Use a 7¹/₂-ft. leader tapered to 4x.

For both options: Use a 2-ft. tippet of 5x.

For option 1: Use a weighted nymph like a bead-head pheasant tail.

For option 2: Use a lightly weighted nymph like an orange scud.

For option 2: Place 1 to 4 size-B split shot above the tippet knot to get the fly to the right depth.

lure, but they work great as a strike indicator. They are round and made of cork. Other indicators made out of foam look similar, and they also work well, but aren't very durable. Because they are made of real cork, Corkies are very durable, and are available in many colors.

I know two good ways to rig a Corkie as an indicator. You can thread your tippet through the hole and slide it up the leader to where you want it. Then stick a toothpick into the hole and break it off. This will snug the indicator in place. Another way is to first decide where you want the indicator to be on your leader, double-up the leader at that spot and thread the doubled portion of your leader through the hole in the indicator. Then run the tippet and the rest of your leader through the loop until it is pulled tight.

Rig options

There are many ways to rig for nymph fishing. The following are a few setups that work for me. Depending on the conditions, you may want to vary the length or diameter of the leader and tippet. The specs that I list are a guideline only.

However you rig up, think about what you are trying to accomplish. You want the fly to get down deep quickly, and have an indicator in place that you can see and will instantly show when a fish has taken your fly. The rig must also be easy to cast. The lighter the tippet, the more quickly your fly will sink and, possibly, the more strikes you will get. Lighter tippets will result in more flies lost to snags or mean fish, though, so try to find a balance.

Similarly, a long leader and tippet can give you a more

stealthy approach for spooky fish, and will get your fly deeper, but can be awkward to cast.

• To use my basic nymphing rig, start out with a 7¹/₂-ft. leader tapered to 4x. Add about 2 ft. of 5x tippet with a surgeon's knot. Tie a weighted nymph, like a bead-head pheasant tail, to the end of the tippet. Place your indicator on the leader above the tippet knot at a distance approximate to the depth of the water you will be fishing.

If you fish with this style of rig, be sure to use an indicator that is easily moved so you can adjust for different depths. I use this rig only if I'm fishing on a very small stream or in shallow riffles.

This basic rig starts to become impractical if the water you are trying to fish is over 4 ft. deep. You may also find situations where the water changes depth quickly in the space of one cast. You may find a riffle that drops off from 1 to 3 or 4 ft., or more, in the span of 20 ft. Another rigging system would be more practical in this situation. I usually want my nymph to be drifting right in the fish's face, not over its head.

• The next way that I may rig up works in a wide variety of circumstances. Whether the water is deep or shallow, fast or slow, my rig will work. With this setup, I change the amount of extra weight on my leader, not the height of the indicator, to adjust for different current speeds or depth.

I start with the same 71/2-ft. leader, tapered to 4x. I then tie on a 2-ft. tippet of 5x. A lightly weighted nymph, like a scud, goes on the end of the tippet.

Rarely do I find myself fishing in water shallow or slow enough to allow me to effectively fish without any additional weight on my leader. For weight, I almost always have a size-B split shot pinched onto my leader just above the tippet knot. There are times when I might put on two, three, or even four shot to get my fly down in deep, turbulent water. It really works best if you put the split shot on above the

tippet knot so the shot can't slide down to the fly.

The combination of a relatively heavy weight and a lightly weighted fly makes the weight drift along the bottom, bouncing off rocks, while the nymph rides slightly higher—just above the bottom, and right in front of the fish.

I place my indicator near the top of my leader, about a foot from the flyline. Remember, for an indicator to really work, you have to be able to see it. The bigger it is, the easier it is to see. And the closer the indicator is to the tip of the flyline, the easier it will be to cast. A big indicator is the size of a bass popper, and you will be able to turn it over on your forward cast if you keep it near the flyline.

Again, specific circumstances can require changing the length or diameter of your leader and tippet. A big nymph, like a #6 stonefly, requires a heavier tippet. A small nymph, like a #18 brassie, calls for a lighter tippet.

Sometimes, when I tie on my tippet, I leave the heavier of the two tag ends from the knot untrimmed. If the water is very snaggy, I put my split shot on this tag end. If the shot gets snagged, it will pull off, and I

won't lose my fly and tippet. Also, if I want to fish with two nymphs at once, I can tie my second nymph onto this same tag end. (More on fishing with two flies later in the chapter.)

• In shallow, snaggy water, you can minimize snags by substituting moldable soft weight for split shot. Moldable weight isn't as heavy as shot, and it drifts through rocks instead of grabbing them. Place the moldable weight on the leader-tippet connection to keep it from sliding.

With my nymphing system, it is possible to keep your fly drifting along the bottom in virtually any situation by varying the amount of weight, not the position of your indicator. Even if the water gets deeper as your nymph drifts along, it will stay right down near the bottom.

Casting strategies

Nymph fishing usually requires that you fish upstream. Start by positioning yourself at the downstream end of a likely-looking riffle or run. Try to imagine exactly where a fish is most likely to be holding. Trout will often hold along the edges of the fastest water, waiting for nymphs to drift by.

Look for current seams in riffle areas. They make good feeding lies; trout hold in the slower water at the edges of a seam (arrows) and pick off drifting insects.

How to Fish a Nymph and Indicator

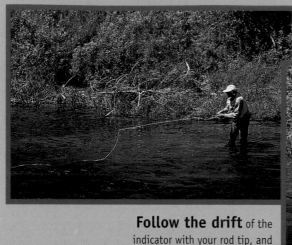

Cast upstream of the water you want to fish. The shorter the cast, the more control you'll have over the drift of the fly.

Follow the drift of the indicator with your rod tip, and mend the line as necessary.

Work out a comfortable amount of line, and cast so that your entire rig lands at least several feet upstream of where you think there could be a fish. You need to land the rig upstream of the fish so the nymph has a chance to sink to the bottom by the time it gets to the fish.

As soon as your cast lands, you must immediately regain control of the line by capturing the flyline with the front two fingers on your rod hand. Keep your rod low while you do this. You will need to start stripping in line immediately, fast enough to keep up with the current. Reacting too slowly will result in slack line, called a "belly." If you get a strike while in this position, you won't be able to take the slack out of the line on the hook set, and will almost surely miss the fish.

Watch the indicator closely while you strip in line, and set the hook by sharply lifting up on the rod tip if the indicator goes under, stops, or does anything else suspicious. Try to visualize exactly where your fly

is and what it is doing as you watch the indicator. Remember that your nymph is not directly under the indicator, but several feet upstream of it.

You will probably have many false alarms caused by your fly or weight hitting the bottom, and this is normal. If you give yourself a reason to set the hook on each cast, though, you will definitely catch more fish. Your weight hitting a rock causes your indicator to behave almost exactly the same way it would if a trout ate your nymph. When in doubt, set the hook!

When you do set the hook, one of three things will happen.

• The first possibility is that it wasn't a fish, just your fly or weight hitting the bottom. When you set the hook, your line and leader will go back over your shoulder, forming a backcast. Simply make a forward cast, and you're right back in the water.

• The second possibility is that your fly or weight hit the bottom, but when you set the hook, you find that you are snagged.

To free your fly, head to the closest shoreline, and walk upstream until you are above your snagged fly. A gentle upstream tug on the line with your rod tip usually pops the fly loose. If this doesn't work, you can sometimes wade out to the snag, but you will scare every trout in the area in the process.

If you do get your fly out of a snag, be sure to check that the hook is still sharp, and that you didn't pick up any moss or weeds off the snag.

• The third possibility is that when you set the hook, you will be rewarded with a trout pulling back. You'll be glad that you set the hook. Bring the trout in by holding the rod high, and stripping line. Only use the reel to bring in the fish if the fish pulls out enough line to get you to the reel.

You will sometimes be fishing a spot that requires an across-stream cast to get your fly to the fish. Let's say that you want to fish the edge of the fast water on the other side of the stream. Cast so your fly

Current

Upstream mends can be a delicate procedure. They often include letting the slack line slip through your fingers to prevent disturbing the fly.

lands at least several feet upstream of where you think there's a fish. Since the water between you and your fly is moving faster than the water you want your fly to drift through, your line, leader, and fly will be quickly swept downstream unless you quickly mend the line.

In this situation, mend the line after you make the cast by immediately flipping a loop of line upstream with your rod tip. It will take the fast current several seconds or more to push your flyline past your slower-moving leader. Meanwhile, your fly has sunk to the bottom, and is drifting naturally along the far side of the current.

A proper mend will move the indicator slightly or not at all. When your flyline catches up to your strike indicator, you can make another mend to prolong the natural drift of your fly.

You need to watch your indicator the whole time for a strike. You will probably find it easier to get a long, natural drift with your fly if you hold

your rod high. Don't hold your rod tip high; keep the rod horizontal at shoulder height to keep as much line off the water as possible. You'll be glad you're using a 9-ft.rod.

You will also encounter situations where you have slow water between you and your fly. In that case, you need to mend the line downstream so it can keep up with your swiftly moving strike indicator.

Using two flies

Many anglers nymph fish with two flies at once. By using two different nymphs, you give the fish a choice. I used to fish this way a lot, and I found that I usually caught the same number of fish on each fly.

If you are going to try fishing two nymphs at once, be sure that they are totally different. Using a hare's ear and a pheasant tail together doesn't really give the fish two different choices. Using an attractor nymph, like a beadhead prince, with a smaller nymph like a brassie behind it does make

some sense. The fish may notice the flashy prince, but pass it up and munch the brassie instead. The weight of the bead-head fly may also provide enough weight to eliminate the need for extra weight on your leader.

There are many ways to rig for this style of nymphing. The fly that is on the end of your tippet is called the "point" fly, and the one up your leader is called the "dropper" fly.

Start out with a 7 1/2-ft. leader tapered to 4x. Tie on a 2-ft. tippet of 5x. When you trim the tag ends of the knot, trim only the 5x tag. Leave the 4x tag, and tie your dropper fly to it. You want to tie to the heavier tag because it is slightly stiffer, and will hold your dropper fly away from the leader.

Using a dry fly as a dropper fly and a small nymph as a point fly is a very popular way of fishing. It works best if the dry fly is very buoyant, like an elk-hair caddis, a Wulff, or a grasshopper. Rigged this way, your dry fly acts as a strike indicator as well as a tasty treat to surface-feeding fish.

Fishing with two flies at once does have its drawbacks. I find that you get tangled more often with two flies, and you get snagged twice as often. This means more time rerigging.

The last time I fished with two flies I hooked a huge trout that took me 50 yards down the river. When I got caught up to the fish, I found that I had dead weight on the end of the line, not a fish. I waded out to where my line was stuck, and found that my dropper fly was stuck in a log, and the point fly was broken off. Since that day, I've been happy to fish my flies one at a time.

Fishing with Dry Flies

In the last few years, I've fished with dry flies more and more, even on days when it may not be the best technique. I'm not about to become a dry fly purist, but I can't imagine any experienced trout angler who doesn't prefer dry-fly fishing over other styles of fly fishing. Watching a dry fly being slurped by a nice trout is much more visually satisfying that watching a strike indicator get pulled under.

Leaders for dry-fly fishing are often longer and lighter than those used for other fly-fishing. Leaders from 8 to 12 ft. long, tapered to about 5x or 6x will work in most situations.

Blind casting

For dry-fly fishing to be worthwhile, however, conditions have to be right. It would be unusual for me to fish with a dry fly if I don't see trout feeding on the surface with some regularity.

There are, of course, exceptions. Many times on warm summer days, there doesn't seem to be much of anything happening on the trout stream. Even dredging deep riffles and runs with nymphs fails to produce fish with any regularity on some days.

When faced with these conditions, I have found that blind casting various attractor-style dry flies in likely-looking runs and along deep banks can be a fun and often productive way to fish—while I wait for a hatch to start in the evening. I like to cover a lot of water,

working my way upstream, when fishing this way.

I have my favorite flies for fishing this way. I start with a Royal Wulff, size 14, and usually stick with it. I guess that I like the way it looks and the way it floats when treated with a good fly floatant. The fish seem to like it just fine, too. It doesn't really look like any insect in particular, but it is very visible to the fish as well as to me, and it has a generally buggy look. Other similar flies will probably work just as well, like Humpies or Irresistibles.

Another good option is using terrestrials, like ants, beetles, hoppers, or crickets. One of my favorite times to fish this way is after a good rain. When it rains hard enough to wash bugs to the water from the bank and streamside bushes, but not so hard that the water is muddied up too much, the trout will definitely be looking up for an afternoon snack.

On big, western rivers that are often fished from a driftboat, you can drift a big grasshopper along miles of stream bank as the boat floats along. While a friend or your guide rows the boat, you can keep your fly drifting along likely looking banks for a minute or more until you have to recast.

This is also a great time to fish two flies. The hopper/dropper combination has become a very popular presentation, especially out West.

Fly options

I haven't fished for stream trout as much as some folks, but I have done it a lot, and have fished many, many hatches. I have never fished a hatch where one fly caught fish like crazy, and nothing else worked at all. I certainly have had times where one fly did seem to work slightly better, but it's much more typical for constant changing of flies to be required. It's almost like each fish has its own personal tastes as to what it looks for in a meal.

Maybe I would catch just as many if I stuck with the first fly that got eaten. The bottom line is that if you use a fly that is the same size, the same shape, and about the same color as the naturals, you'll get some rises. But having a few other options in your box will get you more rises.

When trout are rising freely and you're using a fly that seems to match the natural bugs, and you still can't get a fish to take your fly, here are some things to try:

• The first thing should be obvious: Try a new fly. If you started with a traditional, high-floating dry fly, change to a lower-riding fly like a thorax or comparadun style. Sometimes, that's all it takes.

• Still no takers? Try lengthening your leader by adding a few feet of tippet, lighter than what you already have on. The longer your leader and tippet are, the easier it is to get your fly to float drag-free.

Drag is caused by your line, leader, and/or tippet moving faster or slower than your fly. You often have to mend your line upstream or downstream to ensure that everything drifts at the same speed. Rarely will a trout take a dry fly that is dragging unnaturally on the surface.

• While I cast upstream, or up-and-across stream most of the time when dry-fly fishing, sometimes a downstream presentation can be a better option, especially on slower-moving sections of a stream.

To make a downstream presentation, carefully and slowly position yourself a comfortable casting distance above the fish.

If the fish is rising 30 ft. below you, have about 40 ft. of line stripped off your reel. When you make your cast, check it so the fly lands quietly a few feet above the fish. Feed line out as the fly drifts away from you and toward the fish.

When you make a downstream presentation, you aren't casting over the fish, and the fish will see your fly before it sees your leader or line. If the fish doesn't take it, let your fly drift well past it before making a new cast.

Casting Upstream

Upstream casts should be slightly across the stream's current to keep the line and tippet from spooking the fish.

Stripping speed is crucial—too quick puts drag on the fly, and too slow allows extra slack to gather near the rod tip.

Fishing with Streamers

I have always liked fishing for trout with streamers. While most streamers are tied to imitate small fish, like minnows, sculpins, chubs, or small trout, some look more like leeches or crayfish.

Streamer fishing for trout requires a much more active approach than other styles of trout fishing. When streamer fishing, you search for only the biggest and most active trout.

To be successful in streamer fishing, you almost have to forget everything else you know or have heard about trout fishing: Forget matching the hatch, natural drifts, and light tippets. It might help if you pretend that you're fishing for pike or bass.

Conditions

When I was a kid, I used to fish for trout on a regular basis with Mepps spinners and small Rapalas on a light spinning rod. On some days, these lures worked so well that I thought if

people knew what I could catch on them, they'd outlaw them. On other days, though, it was a very long time between strikes.

The conditions when these lures worked so well were almost always the same: It was usually on days when the water was off-colored from recent rains, or on dark, overcast days. On bright, sunny days when the water was clear, the trout almost always ignored or spooked away from the flashing or wobbling lures.

What does this have to do with streamer fishing? Everything!

Streamers have a lot in common with lures fished on a spinning rod. Both are most likely to be attacked by active fish.

On an overcast day, or when the stream is flowing slightly off-colored, a large percentage of the trout could be considered to be active. When the skies are high, and the water is clear, a large percentage of the fish are likely to be inactive, and unlikely to chase down a lure or a streamer.

I usually reserve my streamer fishing for days when the conditions tell me the fish will be active. Although streamers will catch trout of all sizes, if conditions look good, I head for water known to produce big fish.

I use a slightly heavier rod for streamers than I normally use for trout fishing, like a 6-weight. A 5-weight will work, but go any lighter and you'll have trouble casting a large fly. And a large fly is what you should be using. Remember that you're trying to catch active and/or large trout.

A large fly will trigger these fish better than a small one every time. How big? I hesitate to recommend hook sizes, because streamers are tied on hooks that vary greatly in length, but the overall length of your streamers should be between $1^{1}/_{2}$ in. for streams where trout over 12 in. long are unlikely, and as big as 4 in. where a 20-in. or bigger trout is a possibility.

Setup

I have never been afraid to sling a big fly in most trout streams. A weight-forward floating line will work fine in many situations, but a line with a clear, slow-sinking tip will always work better. In large streams, or anytime you want your fly to get down deep, a line with a 5- to 10-ft. fast-sinking tip is best.

No matter what line I use, I keep my leader as short and heavy as possible. Active trout looking for a large meal are not leader shy. If you're using a floating line, tie on a 7½-ft. leader tapered to 3x; make it heavier if you're using extra-large streamers.

Lighter tippets do not tie securely to a large hook eye, and the knot is most likely to fail on a big fish. You are trying to catch a big fish, aren't you? With a clear tip, shorten the length of the leader to about 5 or 6 ft., and with a fast-sinking tip, about 4 ft. is all you need or want.

Casting strategies

The easiest way to present a streamer is using the down-and-across method described earlier in this chapter: Make an across-stream cast, let the fly swing in the current until it is below you, take a step down and repeat, covering lots of water.

There's usually no mistaking a strike; it's a pretty good yank. Sometimes, though, when a big trout hits a streamer, it comes straight at you after it eats the fly. You feel a small "tick" on the line, then nothing. Again, when in doubt, set the hook.

It isn't uncommon to have what seemed like a good strike, only to miss the fish. This used to drive me crazy, to the point where I even tied flies with an extra hook hanging off the bend of the main hook. I've since decided that most, if not all, of

the missed strikes on streamers are from small trout. Even when using streamers over 3 in. long I've caught 6-in. trout.

Another way to present streamers is to use an upstream presentation. This is more difficult and tiring to do than the down-and-across method but, particularly on small streams where approaching a spot from above isn't advised, it is deadly.

To fish a streamer upstream, make a long upstream cast, as far as you can. As soon as your line and fly hit the water, start stripping in line as fast as you can. You want the fly to appear to be swimming downstream, so it must be moving faster than the current.

Strip the fly in all the way, make a step or two upstream and repeat. Keep moving! In areas with very fast current, it is almost impossible to strip faster than the current is moving, but do your best. When a trout responds to a streamer fished this way, it can easily overtake it, so missed strikes are rare.

Location

When I'm specifically trying for big trout, I concentrate on high-percentage spots. Riffles and runs that flow into a deep hole are prime areas. During low-light periods, or when the water is off-colored, big fish that spend most of their time in the deep holes move into shallow areas to feed.

Tail-outs found below a deep hole are also prime areas. It was in such a spot that I caught my biggest-ever stream trout. It was a rainy morning in May. I was on a small stream in Wisconsin that has a reputation for producing big fish, over 10 lbs. I was using an 8-weight rod and a 4-in. wool-head sculpin for a fly. The water

clarity was less than 2 ft., so conditions were prime for big fish.

At the tail-out of a deep corner hole, a tree was caught on a boulder in the middle of the stream. I made a cast that would bring my fly right into the tree. My line stopped dead right when my fly should have gotten to the tree. I thought I had gotten snagged on the tree, but I set the hook anyway. Instead of a snag, I was hooked up to a big trout!

My stout rod and heavy leader enabled me to get the fish in quickly. It wasn't a 10-pounder, but it was almost 2 ft. long and probably weighed about 5 lbs. That was one fish that wouldn't have been caught if I hadn't been specifically trying to catch a big trout.

As soon as your line and fly hit the water, start stripping in line as fast as you can. You want the fly to appear to be swimming downstream, so it must be moving faster than the current.

Trout in Lakes

Fly fishing for trout in lakes doesn't get as much press as fishing for them in streams. Maybe it's because fishing for trout in a lake doesn't have the visual appeal that fishing in a stream does. It could be because trout in lakes are often easier to catch than their stream-living counterparts. Or maybe it's because trout in lakes can get much larger than trout in streams, and anglers are afraid of them.

Lakes that hold good populations of trout can be found throughout Canada and the northern and mountain U.S. states, including each of the five Great Lakes.

Most trout in lakes are there as a result of stocking. Since trout generally require flowing water to spawn, natural reproduction isn't an option unless the lake has a stream flowing in or out of it.

Trout fishing in a lake generally requires the use of watercraft. I usually use a float tube because it is quiet and easy to transport to backwoods lakes.

There are opportunities on some lakes to catch fish by wading, especially in the spring and fall, when cool surface temps allow the trout to roam the shallows, searching for food. But to be really serious, you should be fishing from some kind of watercraft. That will enable you to fish the shallows as well as deeper water. In the summer, the majority of the trout will be in deeper water.

Location

When I head out from shore in my float tube on a trout lake, I pay attention to water clarity, weeds, and bottom type as I fin toward deep water, and I'm always on the lookout for rising fish. It can be hard to pinpoint exactly where the trout will be in a lake; they often roam over deep water, out from the weedlines. So whenever I see fish rising, I head in their direction. One trout rising will often reveal the location of a concentration of fish.

Technique

I approach to within comfortable casting distance of where I saw a trout rise, and start casting. Even when trout are feeding on the surface, they still respond well to flies fished below the surface. And even though I saw a fish rise, I still allow my line and fly to sink for a few seconds before beginning my retrieve. I make the retrieve by stripping line in short, 6-in. pulls. When you get a strike, sometimes you'll feel a good jolt; other times the line will just tighten up as you make your retrieve. As always, when in doubt, set the hook.

If there is a hatch in progress, and you see fish rising with regularity, you'll want to use a floating line and a dry fly that approximates the natural bugs you see on the water. When a good hatch is on, and lots of bugs are floating on the surface, a trout will often cruise just below the surface, picking off bugs as it swims along.

Setup

You can use the same rod for fishing trout in lakes that you use for fishing in streams. I usually opt for a fast, 9-ft. 5- or

6-weight, but a lighter rod will work fine, especially on calm days or for fishing dry flies.

You can do a lot of trout fishing in streams with only a floating flyline, but on lakes, it's a different story. If you use only a floating line on a lake, you'll be limited to fishing the top 4 ft., and there are just too many times when the trout are deeper. At least one sinking line should be with you whenever you venture out on a trout lake. A floating line with a 10-ft. sinking tip will enable you to get a fly down to around 6 or 7 ft., and a full-sinking or integrated-head line will easily get you down 10 ft. or more.

Flies

Trout in lakes eat many of the same things that trout do in streams. Damsel and dragonfly nymphs are also regularly on the menu for trout in lakes in many areas; so are scuds, mayflies, leeches, snails, water beetles, midges, caddis, and minnows. You should have some imitations of at least a few of these before you venture out.

If I had to pick one fly, it would be a wooly bugger, black or olive, size 6 or 8. I am confident that this fly will catch trout on virtually any lake. A bugger is usually what I start with, and I rarely find a reason to change.

Damselfly Nymph

Wooly Bugger

Sometimes, the fish seem to want something smaller. Then I switch to a hare's-ear nymph, a scud, or a zug bug, usually a size 12 or 14. In some lakes,

Zug Bug

Brassie

midges hatch in huge numbers. Even though the bugs can be tiny, fish feed heavily on them, and a midge larva imitation, like a brassie, often gets a good response.

Strike indicators

Trout in lakes can also be caught by fishing a nymph under a strike indicator.

Long leaders and tippets are the rule for fishing with an indicator in a lake. I say indicator, but because of the way you'll end up using it, we might as well just call it a bobber.

To rig up, start with a 7½-ft. leader tapered to about 3x. Add some lighter tippet material. How light depends on the size of the fly. The length depends on how deep you want to fish your fly. Have your indicator in place at the bottom of the tapered leader.

To use this rig, just cast it into the area you think has fish, and wait. Occasionally, give the fly some action by twitching your rod tip. When a fish takes the fly, the indicator will either move sideways or disappear altogether.

Casting strategies

Try to cast your dry fly so it lands a few feet ahead of where you think the fish is, in the direction that you think it's headed. After you cast, just let the fly sit there. If you land your fly in front of a few fish and they all ignore it, the next time, give the fly a tiny twitch as a fish approaches.

If you still have no takers, you have a couple other options: blind casting and trolling.

• If you don't see any surfacing fish, you need to start blind casting. If the lake has weeds, just off the edge of them is a good place to start. In cool weather, the fish also cruise the tops of the weedbeds. If the water is clear, you can usually see the weeds, especially if you're wearing polarized sunglasses and it's a sunny day. I always have a flasher-style depth finder on my tube that shows me exactly where the weeds are, and where they end.

If there are no weeds, try fishing near obvious shoreline points or steep breaking shorelines.

• If blind casting doesn't produce, you can try trolling to locate fish. While not technically fly fishing, trolling with a fly will enable you to cover a lot of water quickly, and hopefully locate some active fish. A sinking line works best. Just cast about 50 ft. of line out behind your tube, let it sink, and start finning along.

If you're fishing from some other type of watercraft, use paddles, oars, or an electric motor to move yourself slowly along. Trout are more spooky than other fish in lakes, so be sure to be as quiet as possible. If you hook a fish while trolling, thoroughly work the area by casting.

Experiment with letting your fly sink to different levels. Start by letting your line and fly sink for ten seconds before you start your retrieve. After trying a ten-count for a few casts, try counting to twenty, then thirty, until you determine the level of the fish. Or use a depth finder.

Chapter 11

Largemouth Bass

I've heard that largemouth bass are the most popular gamefish in North America. They are found in every state except Alaska, and the fact that in most lakes they spend their time in shallow water makes them a favorite quarry of fly anglers across the country.

A classic fly-fishing image is that of an angler on a calm morning, working the edge of a lily-pad field for largemouth bass with a popper.

Long before there were bass boats, super-braid line, plastic worms, GPSs, depth finders, and most of the other things that anglers on the pro bass-fishing circuit rely on, people were catching largemouth bass like crazy on flies. Don't get me wrong, I'm a big fan of modern advances in angling, especially in the fly-rod and flyline departments. I have a great time racing around a big lake from spot to spot in a big sparkly bass-fishing boat. If all my fishing was fly fishing for largemouth bass, though, I'm pretty sure I could eliminate most of the modern paraphernalia and still catch lots of fish.

Poppers

Poppers are flies that float on the surface, and have a flat or cupped face that make a popping or chugging sound when you strip them in. Divers are flies that actually dive a few inches under the water when stripped in, and float back to the surface when you stop. While technically different than poppers, they are often fished in the same places and in the same way as poppers.

While bass do bite on poppers of all sizes, it's best to err

on the large side. A bass has a huge mouth, and it uses it to catch and eat large food items like other fish, crayfish, and frogs. A 3-lb. largemouth can easily eat an 8-in. perch. That doesn't mean that you have to throw a huge fly, but you should use something that comes pretty close to the size of what the fish are used to eating.

Most of my largemouth bass poppers are 3- to 4-in. long, but some are longer. If you plan on using a light fly rod, like a 5-weight, you will be seriously limited as to how big a fly you can cast.

Weed guard

Largemouth bass will almost always be found in, or at least near, some form of cover. They lie in the shade that the cover creates, waiting for an unsuspecting baitfish to wander by. It is in your best interest to get your fly as close as possible to the cover, so most of your largemouth flies should have some sort of weed guard. Keep in mind that a weed guard will not guarantee you won't get

hung up occasionally.

The most commonly seen weed guard is made of a loop of heavy mono. This type of guard does a good job, especially in sparse cover. Some flies designed specifically for fishing in very heavy cover come with two mono weed guards.

Mono weed guards of all types are great because they are always in position, and still allow a good hook set. Another style of weed guard is made of thin, single-strand wire. When in place, it protects the hook from all types of snags. However, the wire guard can sometimes pop out of position. If you cast into heavy cover with the wire weed guard out of position, getting snagged is a sure thing.

Material

Bass poppers can be made of several different materials. Most poppers are made of cork, foam, or clipped deer hair. All of them have advantages and disadvantages.

• Foam poppers are used today by more bass anglers than any other material. Foam is

Largemouth Bass Range

Largemouth Bass

Foam Popper

Deer-hair Popper

Cork Popper

Poppers have a cupped or flat face that produces a popping sound when the fly is twitched. They have bodies of foam, cork, or deer hair. Popper weed guards are commonly made of wire or nylon.

cheap, comes in many colors, and is easy to make into a variety of popper shapes. The fact that it floats very high, and keeps on floating no matter how long you use it can be an advantage. Sometimes I think that foam poppers might actually float too high, causing missed strikes. The light weight of foam poppers does make them easy to cast—very important if you plan on using a light rod.

• Clipped deer-hair poppers are a long-time favorite of many bass anglers, especially me. I like the way they sound when you make them pop—not too loud, just a good "blurp!" I think that the nature of the deer hair creates this sound; it "gives" a little when you pop the fly.

Deer-hair poppers ride lower in the water than other poppers, which makes it easy for the fish to engulf them. The bad thing about deer-hair poppers is that they are high maintenance. You need to give them a good dousing of fly floatant before you use them. Even if you do, they still get soggy after an hour or so of

casting, especially if you're catching fish.

It is very important that you use an aggressive casting stroke when using deer-hair poppers; this will help shake off excess moisture. When your popper does get waterlogged, you can dry it off with a fly desiccant and apply new floatant, or tie on a new one.

• Cork is the traditional popper material. It floats great, is durable, and is easy to shape. Good cork poppers are becoming hard to find, though, as cork prices continue to rise. Cork poppers float better than ones made of deer hair, but not as high as foam ones. If you can find them, cork poppers might be the best compromise between deer-hair and foam varieties.

Color

Bass poppers are available in every color under the sun. Personally, I couldn't care less what color a popper is; if it makes a good pop, I know I will catch fish on it. Most of the commercially available poppers come dressed up with fancy paint

jobs, bug eyes, rubber legs, and other additions that don't add to the fly's effectiveness. When a fish sees a popper, it is usually looking up at it and sees it as just a silhouette anyway.

That said, you must have confidence in the fly to really be successful. Fly distributors and retailers learned long ago that anglers just don't buy ugly flies. I make most of my own poppers, and they are very ugly. I doubt that anyone would even buy one of mine, but I like them and catch lots of fish on them.

The colors of my poppers are usually quite bland, without any eyes, legs, or smiley faces. Whenever I take someone bass fishing with me, I let them choose between one of my own plain poppers and a fancy store-bought one. Ten times out of ten, they pick the fancy one. And they probably would catch more fish on the fancy fly than on one of mine, because since it looks good to them, it must look good to a fish, and they fish with more confidence, expecting a strike at any second. If you have no confidence in your fly, you won't be expecting a strike anytime. You won't cast as well, or pay enough attention to what you're doing.

So when you shop for bass poppers, by all means, buy the ones that look good to you, but remember what's most important: They must make a good "pop." Sometimes you will buy a fly that looks great, but just doesn't pop right. You should immediately discard any poppers that don't work correctly.

Hooks

Another thing to pay attention to on your bass flies is the hook. Make sure that the hook is big enough. Even a 12-in. bass has a huge mouth, so most bass flies are tied on hooks that range from a #2 to a #2/0. The hook point should be far enough away from the popper body so there's enough clearance for a good hook set.

Also pay special attention to how sharp the hook is. A bass' mouth is very hard, and using a super-sharp hook will help penetrate it. Luckily, many bass flies available today are tied on chemically sharpened hooks, such as those made by Tiemco or Daiichi.

How sharp is sharp enough?

The old thumbnail test works well. Drag the hookpoint across your thumbnail; if it sticks, you're good to go. If it easily drags across the surface, you need to sharpen it.

If you think your flies need to be sharpened, you can use a small file or a stone. Try to sharpen each side of the point evenly first, then hit the inside of the point. Take your time, because once you remove metal from the hookpoint, you can't put it back. You might want to practice sharpening on an old, beat-up fly, or even a plain fish hook.

Poppers take more largemouth bass than any other fly.

Setup

If you're serious about large-mouth bass fishing, an 8-weight rod is as light as I would go. I use a 9-weight most of the time, and a 10-weight isn't out of the question if the bass are big and the cover heavy.

Besides casting a bulky fly better, a heavy rod gives you needed hook-setting and fish-fighting power. When you factor in the big flies bass like to eat, their hard mouth, and the heavy cover they live in, a heavy rod is the best choice.

There are always exceptions. For instance, there's a lake near my home with a huge popula-tion of small largemouth bass. Most of the bass in this lake are less than 2 lbs., and are often found around sparse, submerged weeds. Since I usually cast smaller poppers when fishing this lake, I find that a 7- or even a 6-weight is completely adequate, and I could probably get by with a 5.

Your fly reel should be the right size to match the weight of the rod. While even the biggest bass in the lake won't run out your whole flyline and take you into the backing, you should still load the reel with as much backing as possible before putting on your flyline to prevent it from being stored in tiny coils.

Your flyline should be a floating bass-bug taper. While a standard weight-forward line will work, a bass-bug line's beefed-up taper really does cast a big fly better. It also has a finish that is formulated to per-form best in warm weather, which is when you'll be most likely to go bass fishing.

What you choose to use for a leader is very important. The heavier and shorter your leader is, the easier it is to cast a big fly. In many types of fly fishing, some finesse is required. Popper fishing for bass is not one of these types. I haven't found a situation where bass are leader shy, so I never use a leader with less than a 10-lb. tippet. If I am fishing in very heavy cover, I might use as much as 20 lbs. for a tippet. The overall length should be no more than 8 ft., and I sometimes use leaders as short as 4 ft.

There are leaders made specifically for bass fishing, but if you can't find any, get the shortest, heaviest trout leaders you can, like a 7½-ft. tapered to 1x or 0x. Knotless leaders are greatly preferred for bass fish-ing because knotted leaders tend to pick up bits of algae and weeds on the knots.

Location

Now that you are set up with the proper outfit, some heavy leaders, and a good selection of flies, it's time to catch some bass! Before you can catch them, though, you have to know where to find them. Where you should begin your search for largemouth bass is somewhat dependent on the time of year.

Spring

Where I live, the lakes are frozen until about mid-April, and bass season doesn't even open until late May. This closure of bass fishing is done to pro-tect the fish while they're spawning, which I am in favor of. However, this closed season causes us to miss out on one of the best fishing times of the year: the pre-spawn.

Before the bass actually start to spawn, they feed very active-ly as they cruise shallow bays, the same areas that load up with panfish in the early spring. To get in on this action, you'll have to go to a state that has an earlier opener for bass fish-ing. In most of the country, though, especially in the South, bass season is continuous.

When the water temperature rises into the 60s, largemouth bass begin to spawn. They spawn in pairs. The smaller males create spawning beds, usually near an object like a log or big rock in 2 to 4 ft. of water, and the larger females soon join them. The bass guard their beds against any intrud-ers, including a well-placed fly. The morality of catching bass off their beds is often debated, but most people agree that as long as the fish is immediately released, it will get back to its nest-guarding duties soon enough.

I personally choose not to deliberately catch bass off their spawning beds. That doesn't mean that you can't do it, but maybe after catching a few that way you will want to look for some pre- or post-spawn bass, or switch to panfish or pike.

If you do fish for bass when they're spawning, use a heavy rod and tippet to get the fish in as quickly as possible, and release it as close to the bed as you can.

After the spawn, largemouth bass often scatter into slightly deeper water. Locating concen-trations of fish at this time can be difficult. One day, they seem

When weeds are very thick concentrate your fishing on the weed edges. Sometimes these areas are actually the most productive. But if you just don't have much luck, move to a new location.

to be everywhere, and the next day there are none to be found.

While it can be hard to pinpoint their location at this time, blind casting over weed flats, especially during low-light periods, is usually your best bet. Pay special attention to any openings, or holes, in the weeds, and cover as much water as possible.

Summer

By midsummer, largemouth bass have established themselves in their summer lairs. Some bass go deep. Don't concern yourself with catching them on a fly, at least not at first. Many bass, including big ones, spend their summers in and around shallow-water cover, and casting a weedless popper in these areas is a great way to catch them.

• Emergent weeds, such as lily pads, bullrushes, and cattails, are obvious choices. One nice thing about fishing these shallow weedbeds is that the best fishing often occurs in the middle of the day. Look for emergent weeds that are "clean," without a lot of junk weeds growing among them.

In midsummer some lily-pad fields and bullrush beds are so full of junk weeds that they are impossible to fish with a fly rod. These same junk weeds do provide good summertime cover for largemouth bass, but to catch fish out of them on a fly you will have to concentrate your efforts on the edges. Weeds like milfoil and hydrilla often grow so thick that they form an impenetrable mat on the surface, impossible to fish with even the most

weedless fly.

The deep edge of a weed mat is the easiest to fish, and usually the most productive. Sometimes there will be an inside edge on the shoreline side of the weeds, creating an opening between the weeds and shore. While more difficult to fish, an inside edge can be very productive if the water is deep enough.

• Another productive area to fish in the summer is mid-lake humps. These areas are often marked on good lake maps, and on a sunny day, you can easily spot them using polarized sunglasses. On an overcast day, you will have to rely on your depth finder to locate them.

I like to fish mid-lake humps that have good weed growth to within a few feet of the surface. Fishing a popper or diver over the top of these humps is a great midsummer technique, especially during low-light periods.

• Some lakes have little or no weed growth, even in midsummer. This often happens in southern reservoirs. Weeds are always a largemouth bass' favorite form of cover, and any weed growth that you can find is better than other forms of cover.

Reservoirs will sometimes have large areas of standing trees, leftover from before the lake was formed. Bass use standing trees as cover if nothing else is available. The best trees have horizontal underwater branches, providing overhead cover.

On many reservoirs, the trees were leveled before the lake was formed, or they may have long since decayed and fallen down. In this situation, look for shorelines that drop off quickly, and cast to fallen trees, boat docks, or anything else a bass could hide under. Bluffs that drop off into very deep water often hold fish, even without any additional cover. These areas are best during low-light periods.

Fall

As summer turns to fall, largemouth bass fishing remains good, and sometimes gets better. In the fall, largemouth bass start to roam as their summertime shallow-water weedbed homes begin to die off. The shallow weeds that stay green still hold fish, but the best action is often had by blind casting over slightly deeper water where the weeds stay green longer. Poppers can still be effective at this time, but big streamers can often work better.

Reservoirs and bass fishing go hand in hand, especially if there are still standing timber or fallen trees near steep shorelines.

Watercraft

Virtually all largemouth bass fishing is from watercraft—sometimes a float tube, and sometimes a fishing boat like a jon boat or bass boat.

One of the most important aspects of fishing from a boat that is usually not discussed is boat control. No matter how you're fishing, keeping the boat where you want it is critical for success.

Using an electric motor is the easiest way to maintain boat control. There are many subtleties of boat control that I won't get into, but the most important thing to keep in mind is that you should always try to work into the wind. That way, you'll never be moving too fast, or get blown into an area you haven't fished yet.

If your boat doesn't have an electric motor, boat control is more difficult, but you can do okay by starting upwind of an area you want to fish and drifting through with the wind.

You can use your big motor or oars to correct your drift as you go through.

If you will be fishing from a float tube, pontoon boat, or canoe, you will be sitting while fishing. You'll find it much easier to cast if you position your boat so that you are casting across your body.

In a float tube or pontoon boat, you will be traveling backward, so if you're a right-handed caster you should work around a lake counter-clockwise. In a canoe, you will be moving forward, so traveling around the lake in a clockwise direction is best.

Cover

Let's say that you have your boat positioned a comfortable casting distance from the edge of some good-looking cover, such as lily pads. Cast your weedless popper just into the pads. Let the fly sit still for a few seconds and give it a good pop. While any kind of strip on the line or twitch of the rod tip will cause the popper to make some noise, using the line and rod together will really make your popper "talk."

This is easiest if you are standing up in a boat, but you can make it work if you are in a tube or canoe, too: Have your rod pointed out in front of you, about halfway between horizontal and the point where your rod tip would touch the water. You want the rod tip to stay low throughout the retrieve.

Heavy cover

For fishing around heavy cover, a slow retrieve with long pauses between pops is usually best, but it pays to experiment.

As you work your way across the front of the lily pads, pay special attention to any features that are different—a point, an open pocket, or maybe a small clump of bullrushes on the edge of the pads.

If you don't get bit on the edge of the pad field, you may want to work through it again, this time keeping the boat just outside the pads, and casting farther in.

If you are fishing some other kind of cover, such as downed trees or docks, start by first casting along the deeper portions of the cover. Sometimes, you need to make several casts to the same spot to lure the fish out of the cover. A slow retrieve is usually best.

When a bass eats your popper, first strip in line until you feel the weight of the fish. Once you can feel the fish, lift up hard with the rod. You really can't set the hook too hard in this situation. Sometimes the bass will miss the fly on its first try. That's why it's important that you strip in line until you feel the fish before setting the hook with the rod; that way, if the fish didn't get the fly, the fly will stay in the water in front of the fish, giving it a second chance to catch it.

If you hook a bass in heavy cover, you better strip in line very fast and very hard. This is no time to "play" a fish. Keep your rod tip high, and try to keep the fish on top of the weeds until you have it in open water. If the bass becomes buried in the weeds—and many of them will—you'll have to go in after it. However, pulling with your fly rod on a bass buried in weeds is a good way to break your rod.

As quickly as you can, get your boat into the weedbed where you think the fish is buried. Once there, set down the rod, grab your leader, and pull in the fish by hand, weeds and all. When you have the fish close, grab it in the classic way by sticking your thumb in its mouth and grabbing the lower jaw firmly.

Weed flats

If the shallow weeds don't seem to have many fish in them, which can happen in the fall, move out to somewhat deeper water and try blind casting over the tops of weed flats.

Land your largemouth as quickly as possible. Use a landing net if you need to, or grab the bass by the lower jaw to avoid wasting time untangling a lure from a net. If you've located a nice school of fish, you'll want to resume fishing right away.

The best weed flats are ones where the tops of the weeds are about halfway to the surface.

Poppers can still work well on weed flats, but a diving fly like a Dahlberg Diver often works better, and a streamer like a Lefty's Deceiver may work best of all.

At first glance, everything on a weed flat looks the same. If you pay close attention, however, you will notice changes in depth or weed types that can be the key to locating fish. If you hook a fish on a flat, try to remember how deep the water was, and what the weeds looked like where you hooked it. Often you will find other fish located in similar areas.

If you are using a streamer, retrieve the fly by stripping in the line in long pulls. If you get a strike, set the hook the same way you do on a popper.

Anytime from midsummer on, plenty of largemouth bass are found in deep water, usually on the deep edge of the weeds. Depending on the lake, this can be in water anywhere from 4 to over 15 ft. deep.

If the shallow weeds in your lake fail to produce, it could be because there just aren't many fish in the area. Remember, you have to fish where the fish are, and that isn't always where you want the fish to be. Just because a patch of lily pads looks perfect doesn't mean that there have to be bass there.

To fish a deep weedline, position your boat so that you can cast parallel to the weeds. On a sunny day with clear water, you can usually see where the weedline is. If the visibility isn't good enough, you'll have to rely on a depth finder to keep track of the weedline.

The boat has to be stationary—or at least moving very slowly—when you're fishing deep, so don't try it on a windy day. If the weedline is in less than 6 ft. of water, you can use a floating line with a long, 9-ft. leader. For deeper water, a full-sinking or integrated-head fly-line is required with a short, 3- to 4-ft. leader.

My favorite fly for this style of fishing is a weighted weedless, bunny fly, about 4 in. to 6 in. long. To get this fly down deep along a weedline, you have to start out by making the longest cast you can. Then wait about ten to twenty seconds for your line and fly to sink to the bottom. When you think the fly is deep enough, begin your retrieve by making foot-long strips on the line. Largemouth bass respond very well to this presentation.

When you catch a bass off a deep weedline, there will often be more fish nearby. Try to cast back to the same spot, and be careful not to let your boat float over the top of the school.

Dahlberg Diver

Bunny Fly

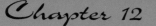

Smallmouth Bass

I have fished for virtually every freshwater fish there is in North America, and quite a few saltwater fish as well. I love the challenge and thrill of catching glamour fish like muskies or steelhead, and fooling a wily brown trout on a tiny mayfly imitation is very satisfying. But for just plain old fun, you can't beat catching smallmouth bass on a fly rod. They will take a wide variety of flies aggressively, and it has often been said that pound for pound, no other freshwater fish fights as hard.

When hooked, "smallies" do pull very hard, and will jump repeatedly in an often-successful attempt to shake the fly loose. When you get a smallie in close and try to land it, it's still

**Smallmouth
Bass**

Smallmouth
Bass Range

usually a long way from done.

Smallies will fight you right until the bitter end every time—while you try to land them, while you take pictures of them, and while you unhook them, they won't miss an opportunity to get you with a spiny fin. And when you release them, they don't just slowly swim away like a steelhead or muskie; as soon as they're back in the water, they are gone in a splash, spraying water on your sunglasses in a final act of defiance.

Location

Smallmouth bass aren't quite as widespread across North America as their largemouth cousins, but are still quite common, especially in the northern and eastern United States. If you live near a river or lake with a good population of smallies, I highly recommend that you give them a try.

Smallmouth bass in lakes often grow bigger than those in rivers, and are often heavier for their length. Last year I fished for smallies on huge Mille Lacs Lake in central Minnesota for the first time, and caught the two biggest smallies I've ever caught.

Wherever you find smallmouth bass, whether it be in a lake or stream, there will almost always be rocks in the area. Smallies may use other forms of cover, like weeds or logs, and sometimes they are even found on bare sand. But there will almost always be rocks nearby.

Smallies like rocks because that's where crayfish live, and smallies love crayfish. When I was a kid, I learned that if you put a live crayfish on a hook and cast it into the vicinity of a smallie, the fish would eat it every single time.

In some bodies of water, especially in mid- to late summer, baitfish like shiners or shad can make up a large portion of their diet, and a big hatch of insects like mayflies can get them looking toward the surface.

Smallmouth bass spawn in pairs like their largemouth cousins. The male will make a nest in 2 to 8 ft. of water with a hard bottom, and it is soon joined by the female. The nest is almost always near an object like a boulder or a log. Smallmouth spawn somewhat later than largemouth do; in my area, smallies can be spawning anytime from mid-May to late June.

If the water is clear, you can easily spot their nests using polarized sunglasses. Smallmouth

will aggressively defend their nests against all intruders. I catch enough smallies during the summer and fall that I personally choose not to fish them while they're spawning, but you can be sure that a fly placed anywhere near a nest will be attacked.

If you're fishing for spawning smallies, use a heavy rod and a heavy tippet. Get the fish in as quickly as possible and release it as near to the nest as possible to ensure that it gets back to its parenting duties.

A couple of weeks after spawning, smallies start to feed aggressively. In rivers, they can be easily caught on flies all summer long. In lakes, especially in the southern portion of their territory, many of the fish go deep, out of range of fly rodders. In northern lakes, though, many fish stay in shallow water all summer and into the fall.

Fall can provide the best fishing of the whole year for smallies. The fact that they feed so aggressively in the fall has prompted the Department of Natural Resources of my home state, Minnesota, to make catch-and-release mandatory for smallmouth bass after mid-September. Good fly fishing opportunities can be had for fall smallies until the water temps drop into the 40s.

Small Streams

I think of small streams as ones that are from 10 to about 100 ft. wide. Most small streams are easily fished by wading, but on the larger ones, floating in a canoe or small boat will enable you to cover much more water. All smallmouth bass streams, small or large, will have plenty of rocks. On some larger rivers, though, you can go for hundreds of yards without seeing a rock. Invariably, when you do find rocks in this situation, you'll find smallies. The good small streams are often very rocky with riffles alternating with deeper pools.

When I fish on a small stream, I usually wade. While I can't cover the amount of water that I could if I floated, the water that I do fish is worked very thoroughly.

Setup

On small streams, I usually arm myself with a 9-ft., 6- or 7-weight rod. My reel has a weight-forward or bass-bug-taper floating line on it.

Having a sink-tip line on a spare spool enables me to get a fly down deep if needed. The leaders I use on the floating line are usually 7 1/2 footers, tapered to 1x or 2x. On the sink-tip, a short 4- to 5-footer tapered to 1x or 2x helps keep my fly right down there with the sunk line.

Poppers & divers

Floating flies, like poppers and divers, are a mainstay of smallie fishermen everywhere, and I couldn't imagine going fishing without some of them in my box.

Since catching smallies on surface flies can't be beat for a good time, I usually start out with either a popper or diver tied to my tippet, as long as conditions allow it. If the water temps are in the 60s or higher, smallies will hit surface flies.

Typically, I start by working my way upstream, casting to any and all likely-looking water, usually along a shoreline. You can skip low-percentage areas, such as the middle of deep pools, or shallow sand flats. You want to look for areas that have as much going for them as possible. Most of the actively feeding smallies will be found in water from 1 to 3 ft. deep with moderate current. Anything that disrupts the current, causing a current break, should get special attention.

The best areas often have deep and/or fast water nearby, and, besides rocks, will have some cover like downed trees or weeds present. You should try to position yourself down- or across-stream of a likely-looking spot, and cast your popper so it lands a few feet upstream of it. As soon as the fly touches down, begin your retrieve.

You should retrieve a popper for smallies the same way you do for largemouth, by using the line and rod at the same time. A steady pop-pop-pop retrieve is usually better than a stop-and-go retrieve for smallmouth, but it pays to experiment. A smallie strike on a surface fly can be explosive, but sometimes it will simply slurp the fly off the surface, leaving hardly a ripple.

However the fish hits your fly, set the hook hard, and strip fast to keep the line tight. Continue to strip in line whenever the fish will allow it. When

you have the fish in close, you can land it by gripping its lower jaw, or scoop it up under the belly. A smallie picked up in this manner will usually stay motionless until you can unhook it.

The average size of the smallmouth bass on a small stream is usually less than what I catch on larger streams and lakes. Since the fish run small, I usually downsize my poppers, using ones that are about 2 in. long.

Remember, though, that just because a body of water is home to a lot of small fish, it doesn't mean that there aren't a few big ones in there, too. This is true for other fish species in other bodies of water as well. To target trophy-size fish, you often have to sacrifice quantity for size, and using the biggest fly that you dare to tie on is usually the best way to do it.

Streamers

Streamers are fished below the surface. Some of my streamers are lightly weighted, and are fished quickly just below the surface. Other streamers are weighted heavily, often with dumbbell eyes to get them down deep. The most common streamer of this type is the Clouser Minnow. The dumbbell eyes tied in at the front of the fly give it a jigging motion when retrieved, and also cause the fly to ride hook point up, reducing snags.

If poppers and divers aren't producing, I change tactics by putting on a sink-tip line and a bottom-bouncing fly like a Clouser Minnow, a Whitlock Hare Sculpin, or one of my own patterns.

Crayfish imitations, of course, can also be successful. When you choose crayfish flies,

Casting across a riffle to set up a drift with a streamer is a great way to catch smallies. On a hot day, you can do it with no vest or waders—if your vehicle is nearby and the water is warm.

try to find ones that will have good movement in the water. Many crayfish patterns that look good in your hand are too stiff, and look more like a stick than a crayfish in the water.

Flies tied with materials like rabbit fur, marabou, and rubber legs flow and pulse when wet. You can get by using your floating line, but a sink-tip works much better.

The easiest way to fish a fly deep is by using an across or down-and-across presentation. Remember that even with a heavy fly and a sink-tip line, it takes at least several seconds for your fly to get to the bottom.

The best place to try catching fish on a sink-tip line is at

Clouser Minnow

Whitlock Near Nuff Crayfish

the lower end of a deep pool, just where it starts to shallow up. Cast across the stream, and allow your line and fly to drift in the current downstream until the fly is directly below you. Take a step downstream and repeat. Sometimes I give the fly extra action by making short

strips on the line or twitching the rod tip, but just letting the fly swing in the current is usually all you need to do.

If the water is too deep or fast for your fly to get to the bottom, you will have to learn how to mend your line. This means repositioning your line on the water after it has been cast to alter the way your fly drifts.

To get your fly deeper, throw a loop of line upstream as soon as your line and fly hit the water. Try to do this without moving the fly. It will take the current several seconds to straighten out this loop of line. Meanwhile, your fly is sinking down to, or at least near, the stream bottom. When fishing in this manner, your fly should tick the bottom occasionally.

Sometimes a strike will just feel like your fly got stuck on the bottom; other times it will be a hard yank. When in doubt, set the hook.

When you're fishing with streamers, losing some flies to snags is inevitable, and I would go so far as to say that if you're not losing at least a few flies, you're not getting your fly deep enough. This is also a good way to catch other fish species. I've caught walleyes, channel catfish, carps, and many others while fishing this way.

Nymphs & dry flies

Round out your small-stream smallmouth fly selection with some nymphs and dry flies.

In some streams, aquatic insects are fed upon heavily by smallmouth, so having at least a few big nymphs and attractor-style dry flies is a good idea.

All of my smallmouth flies are barbless. Now if there's a fish that can rid itself of a barbless fly, it's a smallmouth. Smallies almost always jump when hooked, shaking their head violently from side to side, trying to shake the hook. I used to get mad when one would give me the slip this way; now it just makes me laugh. I've had enough of them shake barbed hooks, including treble-hooked lures on spinning tackle, to accept that some of them are just going to get away. As I mentioned before, I'm a believer in pinching down these barbs.

Rivers

On lakes, navigational hazards like rock piles are usually well marked with buoys and easily avoided. On a big river, you'd better know exactly where you're going if you don't want to wreck something. Even though I may know a fifteen-mile section of a river very well, I still destroy at least one prop per year on a hidden hazard.

Setting up a float trip takes some planning, no matter what kind of boat you will be using. If you plan on fishing for one day, about ten miles of river is the most you want to take on.

After you work out the details of getting your boat in the water upstream and then out of the water downstream,

Get the fly to the bottom in fast or deep conditions by mending the line. Smallies will be all over the fly, and you'll have fun during the fight before landing your fish.

you can get down to fishing.

As with other types of watercraft fishing, good boat control is critical. If there are too many obstacles in the water to have a motor down, my fishing partner and I take turns rowing while the other one fishes. If you are the person rowing, it is important that you don't try to fish until it's your turn. Work on holding the boat a comfortable casting distance from the bank while you drift, and hope that your fishing partner does as good of a job of rowing as you did when you switch places.

It takes at least several trips down the same section of river before you start to get a feel for it. On my home stretch of the Mississippi, almost everything looks like great smallmouth habitat, but I've learned that while I've caught fish almost everywhere, certain areas have just the right combination of depth, current speed, and cover to be consistently productive.

Dropping anchor to thoroughly work an area can be worthwhile, but don't spend too much time on one spot; an actively feeding smallie often hits a fly the first time it sees it. Some spots that might be worth anchoring on are a tributary stream, a large current break, or an isolated rock pile.

Setup

I use heavier tackle when I'm fishing from a boat than I do when I'm wading. Since I'm almost always moving while in a boat, and I want to get casts into as many spots as possible, I use a fast-action 8- or 9-weight rod and a reel loaded with a floating bass-bug taper line and a leader tapered to 0x or 1x. This kind of setup allows me to

cast my fly anywhere I want it to go with minimal false casting.

A heavier rod speeds up the time it takes to get a fish in. There's nothing wrong with having fun playing a fish, but the whole time you're bringing in the fish, other good spots are floating by. Using a landing net on a big fish when you get it to boatside will also speed up the time it takes to get the fish landed, unhooked, and back on its way.

Poppers & divers

On a big river, the water is usually dark. Smallies can have a hard time homing in on their food when the visibility is poor. That's why I like to use a noisy surface fly most of the time. A smallie has no trouble finding a noisy popper or diver.

I look for the same qualities in a popper for smallmouth fishing that I do for largemouth fishing. I use poppers made of foam, cork, and deer hair. Regardless of what the popper is made of, make sure that it pops when you want it to. It doesn't matter to the fish what color it is, but I do like to use ones that I can easily see.

While poppers do work very well, I think that Dahlberg divers are the best surface fly for smallmouth bass in rivers. A properly tied Dahlberg diver makes a great "ka-chunk" sound every time you strip on the line. The way that a diver goes a few inches below the surface and then pops back up is irresistible to a smallmouth.

A smallie will usually whack a diver while it's floating, but sometimes it will grab it underwater, too. Many times when using a diver, I've set the hook into a fish, not because I saw a strike, but because my diver

never resurfaced.

Be sure to give a Dahlberg diver a good coating of fly floatant before it gets wet. Even with floatant, you will probably need to change flies periodically as the deer hair soaks up water.

Streamers

Poppers and divers can still produce when the water is clear in your river, but minnow-imitating streamers are often a better choice.

If I decide to use streamers, I sometimes use the same rod that I use for popper fishing, but I find it to be much more efficient to have a separate rod rigged for streamer fishing. That way, I can quickly change back and forth between the two. You don't always get the explosive strikes when streamer fishing as you do with surface flies. But since your fly is usually just below the surface, you can still see the fish eat the fly.

When the water cools, the number of fish you catch makes up for the lesser surface action.

Bottom-bouncing flies

Fishing a fly right along the bottom is another very productive tactic, but one that I usually save for a when-all-else-fails scenario. Some days, the fish just aren't in the mood to chase anything. Using a heavy fly on a floating or sink-tip line will put the fly right in their face, and will get strikes when nothing else works. Fishing deep is not as much fun as fishing on or near the surface, and sometimes borders on being tedious.

Getting snagged is part of the game, so be sure to have enough flies. Sometimes you can get a snagged fly back by motoring or rowing the boat to a position upstream of the snagged fly. Don't try to get a fly back by pulling on it with the rod from downstream of the snag; your rod may get broken.

If getting upstream of the snag is impossible, point your rod directly at the snag and hold the line tight. Either the fly will come loose or the tippet will break. If you get the fly back, check to make sure that the hook point is in good shape. Re-sharpen the hook or replace the fly if the hook becomes dull.

Snags are minimized by using flies that are tied with dumbbell eyes, such as Clouser Minnows or Near Nuff Crayfish. I usually fish bottom-bouncing flies in areas that I know have fish in them. I make a short, 20- to 30-ft. cast. Depending on water depth and speed, I may make an upstream mend on the line to help get the fly deep. Once I judge that the fly is near the bottom, I retrieve the fly with foot-long hops, with pauses in between.

Fishing tips

As the boat floats along, try to cast as many times as possible. Always be looking ahead for where you'll want your next cast to go. After you fish rivers for a while, you start to get a feel for fishy spots—they have just the right combination of depth, current speed, and cover.

Try extra hard to cast on the downstream side of any rocks, logs, or other current breaks along the shore. A cast to the upstream side of a downed tree looks inviting, but it's easy to get snagged on it if you're not careful. Then you won't get a cast into the sure thing on the downstream side of it.

The area around any feeder stream, even a storm drain, will hold fish of all kinds, especially after a hard rain. Smallies will lie just below these tributaries, waiting for bugs or worms to wash in.

A big boulder sticking out of the water in midstream will almost always have smallies holding in the slack water pocket on the downstream side of it. Casting a popper or other surface fly into this pocket should be a sure thing, right? Wrong. In my experience, I have never had a smallie eat a surface fly from such a spot. I don't know why, but to get strikes from behind midstream boulders, I find that you have to get your fly to the bottom.

I have made cast after cast with a popper below a big rock with no results. Changing to a heavy Clouser Minnow or crayfish fly plunked in the slack water and allowed to sink to the bottom will often get a fish on the first cast. If your river has a lot of mid-stream boulders, it's a good idea to have a separate rod rigged up with a bottom-bouncing fly, so you're not having to constantly change back and forth.

There is also the temptation to always try to cast your fly as close to the bank as possible. If the water right along the shore-line is at least a foot deep, smallies will hold tight to the bank. But if the water is only an inch deep there won't be any fish there, so land your fly out over deeper water.

If you're trying to put your fly tight to the bank and it lands a couple of feet short, don't recast it. If you get in the habit of recasting every time your fly doesn't land exactly where you want it, you won't spend much time with your fly in the water. No matter where my fly lands, I usually bring the fly in about halfway to the boat before I make a new cast.

Lakes

To locate smallmouth bass in lakes, look for rocks. The best rocks are baseball- to basketball-sized, and located in 2 to 8 ft. of water. If you know a lake where the whole thing is filled with rocks like this, it must be a great smallmouth lake!

Try to find areas with good rocks that also have other forms of cover present, such as weeds, fallen trees, or big boulders. Most lakes have shorelines that are mainly sand or muck, with a few rocky areas. The rocks are where the smallies are.

Some lakes, such as those found in the Canadian Shield, can have a lot of slab rock. Unfortunately, slab rock areas rarely have many smallmouth around them, since there is nowhere for their favorite food, crayfish, to hide. In lakes like this, pass by areas of slab rock and look for areas with broken rocks that are the right size. If there is other cover present, so much the better.

Flies

My fly selection for smallmouth in lakes isn't much different than what I use in rivers. I still try to use surface flies whenever possible, both poppers and divers. Smallies will come up to the surface out of even relatively deep water, as long as the water is clear and the surface is calm. I know one lake where fly rodders routinely get smallies on surface flies out of water 15 ft. deep or more.

If surface flies aren't getting you any action, using subsurface flies that imitate crayfish, minnows, or leeches should be your next plan of attack.

A sink-tip line will get your fly down about 5 or 6 ft., and a full-sinking or integrated head line can get it down 10 ft. or more. A floating line will work only if you're fishing in water 4 ft. deep or less.

In a clear lake, you can usually keep track of the depth you're fishing if you're wearing polarized sunglasses. A depth finder will be required if it's overcast or the water is off-colored.

How to fish a subsurface fly depends on what you are trying to imitate. Minnow-imitating streamers should be fished with a fast retrieve, anywhere from just under the surface to a couple of feet above the bottom. If it's a crayfish that you're imitating, think like a crayfish. Let your fly sink to the bottom, and hop it along the bottom by giving 2-ft. strips on the line with pauses in between.

Chapter 13

Northern Pike & Muskies

It is easy to think of pike and muskies as being very similar. They do look quite a bit alike, and are often found in the same waters. Pike and muskies both spawn in the spring in marshy bays, but muskies spawn a little later than pike. Both fish like to eat big things. As far as I'm concerned, that's where the similarities end.

Northern Pike

Fly fishing for northern pike becomes more popular every year, especially in Canada. Anglers who have long enjoyed catching trout, panfish, or bass on flies are realizing just how easy (and fun) it is to tangle with pike on the long rod. I can't think of a fish that responds as enthusiastically to a wide variety of presentations.

There probably isn't a better way to catch a lot of good-sized fish on a fly than to visit a well-known pike lake in early summer, armed with a 9- or 10-weight rod and some big streamers.

Northern pike are found all across northern North America.

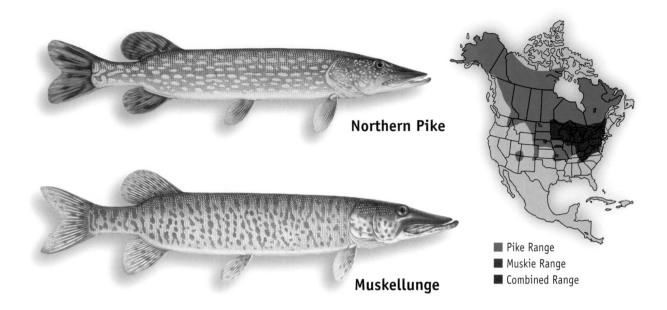

Northern Pike

Muskellunge

■ Pike Range
■ Muskie Range
■ Combined Range

While they can attain huge sizes, the average on most lakes, even in Canada, is less than 10 lbs.

Pike spawn in the spring, just after the ice goes out. They don't make spawning beds like bass, but spawn in pairs or small groups over wide areas in shallow, weedy bays. While some pike stay shallow all summer, most move out to deeper water by midsummer and stay there until the water cools off in the fall. Therefore, your best shot at catching them on a fly is during the cool-water periods. But don't let that stop you from trying in midsummer, especially on a lake with a large population.

If you want to do a full-on assault on some pike with a fly, try late spring, after the spawn, or in the fall, when the water cools and they are feeding actively to fatten up for winter.

Location

As I mentioned earlier, to effectively target pike, especially large ones, with a fly rod, you should try to go during cool-water periods.

Early in the spring, when the water temperatures are in the 50s or cooler, begin your search for pike in or near spawning bays. Look for new weed growth, especially cabbage weed.

During this early season, a slow retrieve may be required if the fish are still recovering from the rigors of spawning. Use a streamer or a rabbit-strip fly that sinks slowly. After you make a cast, let the fly sink for several seconds, then bring it in with 2-ft. strips, pausing briefly between strips.

Once the water warms up to the 60s or more, pike will begin to move toward deeper water and feed very actively. At this time, and for the rest of the year, look for expansive weed flats, the bigger the better. Cabbage weed is the preferred cover for pike, but other weeds like coontail or milfoil will also hold fish.

Work over the top of the weed flat, making long casts and retrieving the fly quickly.

When the pike get active, you can't retrieve the fly too fast. The same streamers and rabbit-strip flies still work.

A Mega-Diver will work across the top of a weed flat, and you can still use a floating line. But as the water warms up even more, most of the fish move out to the deepest weeds. Using either a full-sinking or an integrated-head line will get your fly down to their level.

Using the same technique I described earlier in the book for catching largemouth bass when they go deep will catch plenty of pike, even in the summer. A deadly variation of this technique is to use a floating fly, like a Mega-Diver, with a sinking line.

Make a long cast along the edge of the weeds and let the line sink. When you strip in line, the fly will dive down with each strip, and slowly rise toward the surface when you pause. Any time you are fishing around heavy weeds for pike, you should use a fly with a wire weed guard of some kind.

Setup

Pike have a big mouth that is full of sharp teeth. They use it to catch and eat other fish of all kinds, as well as anything else they think they can. Studies have proven that pike prefer to eat other fish that are approximately one-third their own length. So a 24-in. pike, which weighs about 4 lbs., will ideally try to eat something about 8 in. long. A 40-in. pike, which weighs about 17 lbs., will ideally try to eat something over a foot long! This doesn't mean that you have to—or even would want to—try casting a foot-long fly, but it does show that you really can't use a fly that is too big.

To be really serious about catching pike, you should be using a fly at least 4 in. long; almost all of my pike flies are 6 to 8 in. long. I've used flies even bigger, but they are just too hard to cast.

Since the flies you'll be using will be large, a minimum of an 8-weight rod is required, and a 9- or 10-weight is ideal. You can land a pike of any size on a lighter rod, but you'll be seriously limiting the size of fly you can cast.

Your reel should be the right size for the rod, and be loaded with a pike taper line, which has an even shorter and heavier weight-forward section than a bass-bug taper line does. A pike taper line will make it easier to cast a big fly. But a standard weight-forward line will work.

Leader

One reason more fly anglers haven't tried fishing for pike is probably because of the leaders that must be used. Often, when I mention "wire tippet" to someone who has fly fished only for trout or panfish, they get a scared look on their face, and go back to their brookies and bluegills.

To land pike with any consistency, you must have a piece of wire between your fly and the rest of the leader, or the sharp teeth will cut right through your tippet. It is very possible to land a pike without a wire tippet, and you might even land several in a row with nothing to protect your leader from their teeth. Eventually, though, one will bite through, and the next ten might do the same.

You may be tempted to try using heavy monofilament instead of wire. While that would be better than nothing, you don't want to lose your biggest fish ever because it bit through your line, so use wire!

There are several ways to rig a leader with wire. The easiest way is to buy pre-made pike leaders. Cortland, Scientific Anglers, and Rio all offer different pike leaders with the wire already attached.

• Cortland's pike leader has a heavy monofilament butt section with a foot-long piece of 20-lb., nylon-coated, seven-strand wire attached. You can attach your fly to the wire by using one of the crimping sleeves that come with the leader.

• The pike leaders made by Scientific Anglers have a heavy mono butt section attached to a length of single-strand wire with a snap on the end. All you need to do is snap your fly on, and you're ready to go.

• Rio uses the same heavy butt section, but for wire they use one of the new "knottable" wires. You attach your fly by tying a knot. Several knots will work for this; a three-wrap clinch or a Duncan loop knot are good options.

We sell hundreds of pike leaders every year at the fly shop where I work. That's good for business, but it wouldn't hurt my feelings if everyone would at least try to make their own pike leaders. It's very easy to do (see below), and all you need is a spool of knottable wire and some heavy monofilament. If you know how to make your own pike leaders, you can rerig in a minute.

Flies

It used to be that most, if not all, flies used for pike fishing were actually saltwater flies. Some fly patterns originally designed for saltwater are still used by pike anglers.

• The Lefty's Deceiver is a saltwater streamer pattern designed by Lefty Kreh over forty years ago, and no one has come up with a baitfish imitation that is much better.

How to Make Your Own Pike Leaders

Butt Section   Tippet

Make a leader using a butt section of 30- to 40-lb. monofilament and a tippet of 15- to 40-lb. knottable wire like Surflon Micro Supreme wire made by the American Fishing Wire Company. Use a 4- to 6-ft. butt with a floating line, and a 2- to 3-ft. butt with a sinking line. In either case, the tippet should be about a foot long. Attach the leader butt to the flyline with a nail knot; to the wire with an Albright knot. Attach the fly to the tippet with a Duncan loop or a clinch knot.

• Another saltwater fly in heavy use by pike anglers is the Flashtail Whistler designed by Dan Blanton. Its flashabou tail matched with a heavy collar and bead chain eyes is a combination that brings pike running.

• Larry Dahlberg's Mega-Diver is an over-sized version of the popular Dahlberg Diver bass fly. This fly is one of a relative few designed specifically for catching pike (and muskies). Despite their large appearance, Mega-Divers are still very castable on a 9- or 10-weight rod. Like other divers, they float at rest, and dive a few inches when you strip in line. They are one of the best pike flies of all time, especially for large fish.

• Subsurface flies tied with long rabbit-strip tails have an action that is irresistible to pike and other game fish. When wet, the rabbit fur flows and pulses like a living creature every time you strip on the line. There are many different rabbit-strip flies available, but a few of the best are Barry's Pike Fly and Dave Whitlock's Hare Worm, Hare Grub and Hare Jig.

All of these flies are produced by Umpqua Feather Merchants, and are available across the country. If your local fly shop doesn't have any of these specific patterns, don't worry; pike are not too picky about what they hit. Keep in mind that the number-one pike lure of all time is a red-and-white spoon. I figure that any fish that will hit one of those things with reckless abandon is not too hard to please, and I can't imagine any big streamer that won't catch pike.

Don't worry too much about color, either. I try to use flies that I think will be most visible

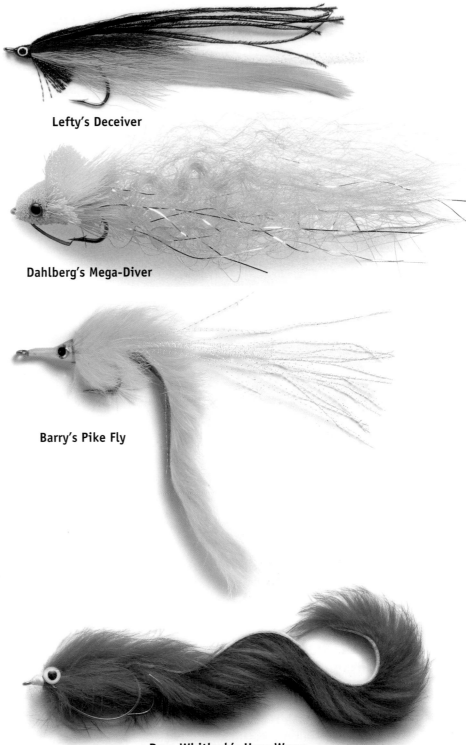

Lefty's Deceiver

Dahlberg's Mega-Diver

Barry's Pike Fly

Dave Whitlock's Hare Worm

to the fish. In most situations, you really can't go wrong with a fluorescent chartreuse fly. This color shows up well under many conditions.

Black is also a very good choice, and so is white. It's fun to mix it up by trying different colors, but if you're not catching pike, I doubt that it's because of the color of your fly.

Be sure to have plenty of flies with you on each pike outing. Even the best-tied fly will be looking pretty ratty after several pike have their way with it.

Accessories

There are a few accessories that are mandatory equipment for pike fishing:

• Always have a pair of needle-nose pliers or another kind of hook-removing tool that will enable you to extract a fly from the back of a pike's toothy mouth. The forceps that you use for unhooking trout or sunnies won't work. A Baker Hook-Out works very well; you can keep your fingers out of harm's way while unhooking the fish.

• You can further protect your hands from cuts by wearing a Lindy fish-handling glove. These gloves are both hook-proof and tooth-proof.

• A Baker jaw spreader can make unhooking a deeply hooked fish much easier. Jaw spreaders keep the fish's mouth locked open while you pop the fly out. They are available in 6-, 8- and 10-in. sizes, and the 6-in. works fine on all but the largest fish. Using a jaw spreader that is too big for the fish can cause damage to the fish, so stick to the small size unless fish over 20 lbs. are a possibility.

• Pinching down the barbs on your pike flies really makes the whole unhooking process much easier on you, the fish, and the fly.

Landing the fish

When a pike hits, you'll know it. Pike almost always turn away after they eat a fly, so you will feel quite a jolt. Stripping hard on the line and lifting up sharply on the rod at the same time will ensure the hook gets stuck, but the way that pike turn away after striking usually forces the hook to bury into the corner of their mouth. Here are three good tips for successfully landing your fish:

• If the pike is a small one, you should bring it in by keeping the rod high, and strip in line as the fish allows it. A bigger fish may pull out quite a bit of line after you set the hook. If it pulls out so much that you have line coming directly off the reel, use the reel to bring the fish in. A big pike may take several minutes to get in. Take your time, and gain line on the fish whenever you can by "pumping" the fish in.

To bring a fish in this way, start with the rod held high and bent. Slowly lower the rod while you reel in line. Don't lower the rod faster than you can reel the line in; this will result in slack line. Next, slowly raise the rod up again without reeling to pull the fish toward you, and repeat the process by lowering the rod and reeling at the same time.

When the fish is close, you can land it in several ways. Pike are notorious for "playing possum," lying next to the boat pretending to be played out, only to make one last mad dash just as you try to grab them. So make sure the fish is finished fighting before you try to land it.

For a small fish, less than 30 in., you can easily grab it behind the head, across the gill covers. (I'm right-handed, and I always grab a pike, or any other fish, with my left hand. That way, I can use my right hand to unhook it.)

Pike of all sizes have very sharp teeth, but the teeth on a small pike can actually inflict more damage than those of a large fish.

If you have your hand in the fish's mouth when it thrashes, you are sure to be bleeding, so use a hook-out tool. And if you're still nervous about getting injuried,

wear a fish-handling glove.

If you fish for pike very often at all, getting sliced is inevitable. I'm not talking life-threatening injuries here, just small cuts. But you should always keep a basic first-aid kit in the boat with bandages, tape, and Neosporin.

• When landing a large pike, grabbing it across the gill covers isn't an option unless you have hands the size of Andre the Giant. You can take the easy way out by using a landing net, but what fun is that? It's much more exciting to hand-land even a big pike.

When you have the fish played out, grab the leader and set the rod down. Grab the fish just ahead of the tail with one hand, and slide your other hand under the fish as far up as you can reach.

Swing the fish into the boat and smile for the camera! Have your fishing partner unhook the fish for you and the fish is easily released, none the worse for wear.

If you are fishing alone, it's probably best to just leave the fish in the water while you unhook it. Grabbing it by a gill cover will give you some control over the fish. If you are right-handed, grab the fish by sliding your left hand just inside its left gill cover. Be careful—pike have gill rakers that are very sharp. While you have the fish by its gill cover, use your other hand to unhook it with your hook-outs.

If all this talk of sharp teeth and gill rakers is making you think that pike fishing isn't for you, relax. I've caught thousands of pike and hundreds of muskies in my life, and all of my fingers are still intact.

• If you are really concerned about safety, use a big landing

Canadian lakes are famous for their large pike. It's not always easy to land a pike, but success comes with knowing the proper way to handle one.

net. When you get the fish close to the boat, it can easily be scooped up by you or your fishing partner in a net. If you decide to use a net, make sure that it is big enough for the fish you're likely to encounter. Your net should have a hoop that is at least 30 in. across, with a deep bag.

Place the net just under the water, and hold onto the bottom of the net bag with the hand that is farthest up the net handle. Lead the fish into the net headfirst. When it is halfway in, scoop it up and let go of the net bag at the same time.

There will likely be a considerable amount of thrashing by the fish once it is in the net. Leave the fish in the water until it quiets down. Now the fish can be lifted into the boat and unhooked.

Muskies

Wherever you find pike, they are generally easy to catch. Most lakes that have pike, have a lot of them. But muskies are another story. A lake that has a population of one muskie per acre is considered to be a good muskie lake.

Once you locate muskies, however, you're still a long way from catching one. While pike usually strike any fly you send their way with great enthusiasm, a muskie ignores most offerings, or sometimes just follows your fly back to the boat. It is their habit of following without striking that keeps diehard muskies anglers coming back for more.

A day in which several fish over 20 lbs. follow only inches behind your fly all the way to the boat should get your heart pumping, and increase your determination to catch one. Why they behave this way, no one knows. Muskie anglers will often rate how successful their day was by how many follows they had. Keep at it, though, and eventually one will strike.

Muskie strikes don't come easy, and even when a muskie does eat your fly, there's no guarantee that you'll get a hook stuck in it. While pike practically hook themselves by turning away from you after they eat a fly, muskies often just sit there after they strike—or worse, they keep swimming at you, making setting the hook difficult.

To make matters worse, a

muskie bites down on its prey or fly with so much force that trying to move the fly in the fish's mouth to get the hook set is almost impossible.

One time, when muskie fishing with conventional tackle, I had a muskie strike a wooden plug about 10 ft. from the boat. I set the hook with the stiff, 6-ft. muskie rod I was using and saw the fish's head jerk 2 ft. toward me as a result. Then the fish opened its mouth and just swam away. Imagine, I hit the fish hard enough to jerk its head to the side, and still none of the tines of the two very sharp treble hooks dug in.

So if muskies are never found in big numbers, are hard to coax into striking, and are very difficult to hook with any kind of tackle, why even bother trying for this fish with a fly? Because catching a muskie of any size on a fly rod should be considered quite an accomplishment.

I know that I've made it sound almost impossible, but catching a muskie on a fly is doable if you put in time on good muskie water, use the right equipment, and have your favorite lucky charm in your pocket.

Well, luck doesn't really come into play when fishing very often. Anglers that consistently catch fish aren't successful because of luck, but because they fish a lot, have good equipment, and know how to use it. Where luck does come into play is when a muskie eats your fly, and the hookpoint happens to stick into a part of the fish's very tough mouth that it can actually bury into when you set the hook.

A typical day of fly fishing for muskies for me involves hours of blind casting with a 10-weight rod and an oversized streamer or surface fly. My muskie lakes have relatively high numbers of fish, so it's just a matter of time before I get a strike. Too often, though, a strike comes when I'm not ready for it. Muskies seem to have a way of striking the second that you're not paying attention. After several hours of casting without action, it's easy to let your mind wander. Invariably, a muskie will strike the second you look away from your fly and at a flock of birds or a passing boat.

The same outfit you use for pike fishing will work for muskies, but I don't think you're being serious with anything lighter than a 9-weight; I almost always use a 10. Double-check that all connections are 100 percent, and that your hooks are as sharp as they can possibly be.

Muskies are available as fly-rod targets all summer and well into the fall. Some muskies do spend the summer in deep water, but lots of them stay shallow. I usually start muskie fishing by casting a big surface fly on a floating line around shallow cover. If this doesn't get me any action, I change tactics by casting a big streamer in slightly deeper water, over the top of a weed flat. What may be the best of all, though, is fishing a Mega-Diver on a sinking line around the deep edge of the weeds.

If you spot a fish following your fly, keep the retrieve going. Speed up the retrieve if possible, and keep stripping the fly all the way back to the boat. Sometimes a muskie will continue to follow the fly at the boat if you keep the fly moving in a big circle or figure-8 with the rod tip. The fish usually won't strike during such a maneuver, though. I find that it's best to remember exactly where that fish came from, and return in an hour or two to see if the fish is in a more cooperative mood.

You're not going to get many chances, so when a muskie hits, you'd better be paying attention. Set the hook by first stripping line hard, and then lifting up on the rod hard. If you get a good hook set, you will be in for at least several minutes of intense fish fighting.

While they're not any stronger than a pike of the same size, muskies fight much more violently, frequently jumping and making short but fast runs.

In the process of trying to catch a muskie, you'll probably be interrupted occasionally by a pike or bass that didn't realize your fly was meant for a muskie. So even though it may take you a while to catch a muskie on a fly rod, you can be sure you'll catch plenty of bass and pike in the process.

Chapter 14

Steelhead

When you hear the word "steelhead," what comes to mind? I picture rushing rivers flowing through deep valleys, shrouded by low-hanging clouds. I imagine the smell of last fall's leaves on the ground, the smell of the earth thawing out from another cold winter. The smell of the river itself, still flowing high from snowmelt. The only snow left on the ground is in spots that never see the sun.

I imagine making cast after cast, covering miles of river. Snags are inevitable, and each time I get stuck, I keep the rod bent in an arc after the hook set I made in vain, watching it for any sign of life. Break off, retie, and cast some more. I also imagine cold weather, cold hands, and cold feet.

I imagine how my own stubborn determination only barely outweighs the unliklihood of my fly actually ending up in the mouth of a steelhead. I imagine how exhausted I am, ten hours after I started, as I take off my waders.

Why would you do this to yourself? It's all for going steelhead fishing!

It took me many trips before I ever hooked a steelhead, and many more before I ever landed one. The first time I hooked one, my fly stopped in the middle of the drift. I set the hook, expecting another snag. Instead of a snag, I was rewarded with a hot fish pulling back on my bent rod hard.

Before I could even get past the amazement that I'd hooked one, the fish shot downstream, went through a log jam and came off. My hands were shaking badly as I checked my rig. Everything was in good shape, and I went back to casting. It would be several trips before I hooked another.

Every time I went steelheading and had marginal or no success, it made me that much more determined that I would get one next time.

Unfortunately, most people go steelhead fishing only once. One trip's worth of being cold, getting snagged, and not catching any fish is enough for most anglers. My advice to you is not to be discouraged if you don't succeed on your first trip; determination and confidence will make each outing better than the one before.

My first experiences in steelhead fishing took place on the streams that flow into Lake Superior. I can now hear someone on the West Coast screaming that the "migratory rainbow trout" that we have here in the Midwest aren't really steelhead; that to be a steelhead, the fish has to have spent time in the salt. Okay, they may not technically be steelhead, but while they don't always behave exactly like their western cousins, they do behave very similarly.

I have found that Midwestern fish respond to presentations I thought would only work on clear, Western rivers. It turns out that some of our midwestern techniques work quite well when used on big-time western steelhead streams, too.

Steelhead

Location

By definition, steelhead are rainbow trout that spend most of their adult lives in the ocean or a large lake. Steelhead move into rivers to spawn. When they run up the rivers depends on the river. Most steelhead fishing takes place in the fall, winter, and spring months. Since almost all of the steelhead fishing I've done has been during cold weather, it would seem strange to me to fish for steelhead when it's hot out. But there are places that have summer runs, like the Deschutes and North Umpqua rivers in Oregon.

Once a steelhead enters a river, it heads upstream until it gets to a suitable spawning area, usually runs or riffles with a gravel bottom. A steelhead, unlike most salmon, can spawn several times in its life.

On some streams, the steelhead may travel hundreds of miles to get to where it will spawn. At the other extreme, many of the streams that flow into the Great Lakes have a mile or less of river before a migrating steelhead hits a waterfall or other barrier.

During their upstream migration, steelhead feed very little, if at all. Some of the strikes you

Steelhead Range

get while fly fishing can be attributed to feeding behavior by the steelhead, but most are more likely because of reflex or territoriality.

When the steelhead start to spawn, the female digs a nest, called a redd, out of the gravel with her broad tail. She is usually flanked by one or more males, which fertilize the eggs as she releases them into the redd. She then does her best to cover the fertilized eggs with more gravel.

The redd, and the fertilized eggs, are abandoned soon after, and the steelhead begin to drift back downstream. On their downstream migration, steelhead are called kelts. They feed more actively now than on their upstream migration. After they hatch, the young steelhead, called smolts, live in the river for up to three years before heading downstream to the lake or ocean.

Coloration

Steelhead can be caught during any portion of their time spent in the stream. By far, my favorite time to catch them is just after they have moved into the river.

When they first come into a river from the ocean or lake, they are bright silver in color, with a dark, almost black, back. During this time the are affectionately referred to as "chromies."

When just in from the ocean or lake, they act almost as if they're looking for trouble, aggressively striking at a wide variety of presentations. It must be the time spent swimming in open water that makes them, for lack of a better term, freak out when they feel a hook stuck in their jaw. When you hook one, its first response is usually to leave the area, faster than you would think is possible for any fish.

Steelhead frequently jump when hooked, and just when you think you've got one beat, it's off to the races again as the fish rockets off downstream. When you're battling a hot steelhead, all of the casts, all of the miles, and all of the snags are instantly forgotten as you wonder who's more tired, you or the fish.

As steelhead spend time in the stream, their colors begin to darken, and they soon start to take on a more typical rainbow trout coloration. When they are spawning, their coloration, particularly in the males, becomes quite vivid. Since steelhead will often spawn in shallow water, they can be easy to spot while on a redd. They are also easily hooked when on a redd; and since you can see them, it is easy to drift a tempting fly right in front of their faces.

When a spawning steelhead is hooked, it usually seems to be more interested in getting back to spawning than anything else, and the battle, while spirited, is usually short lived.

I have hooked my share of steelhead off a redd, and I'm not saying that you shouldn't try. After fishing for hours with no sign of a fish, and then seeing four or five fish in plain sight, I can't blame anyone for giving them a try. Now, however, when I see fish spawning, I choose to leave them alone. I find it more enjoyable to watch how they act while spawning than to try to get one to bite.

If you do fish spawning steelhead, try to target the males. They are usually the most aggressive biters, and if you pull one away from a redd, the others will gladly take his place.

Drift-fishing

As I said, my first experiences in steelhead fishing took place in the streams that flow into Lake Superior, mostly on Minnesota's North Shore. These streams are dark and fast, and most have a waterfall or some other barrier blocking migration near the lake. Traditional fly-fishing techniques are impractical there, so many anglers use their fly rods and reels to drift-fish.

While not really fly fishing in the classic sense, this style of drift-fishing is still one of my favorite ways to fish. When I started steelheading, this was how you fished, period. If you have similar conditions, you may want to try it.

I now use a variety of more widely accepted fly-fishing techniques for steelhead when conditions allow. Any time I'm faced with tough conditions, though, like very cold or very muddy water, I'll be the first to rig up for drift-fishing with a fly rod. Any time the water temps drop below 40°F, drift-fishing is usually the best way to hook a steelhead.

Drift-fishing is widely practiced, especially in the Midwest, and it is effective when conditions are tough (which seems to be most of the time). Here are a couple ways to rig, and where and how to try them.

Setup

Start out with a 9- to 10-ft., fast-action graphite rod, 7- to 9-weight. Your disc-drag reel should be balanced to the rod. Fill the reel three-quarters full with backing.

For line, many anglers still use monofilament, 8- or 10-lb. I use mono when fishing streams that have a lot of deep and/or fast water. Put on enough mono to fill your reel. Or you can substitute a "shooting line" for the mono. A shooting line is basically a 100-ft.-long, thin, level, fly line.

Attach about 8 ft. of 12-lb. mono to the end of the running line with a nail or Albright knot. That's your leader.

Drift-fishing requires the use of more weight than you would ever use when flycasting. For weight, you have the choice of using either split shot or slinky weights, which are great, since they reduce snags.

You can make a slinky by inserting some 3/0 round split shot into a length of parachute cord (or a wide nylon shoelace) and sealing the trimmed ends by pinching them together after melting over a candle.

To rig up with a slinky, hook a snap swivel through the middle of one end of the slinky. You'll probably have to go to a general fishing tackle store to get some. While you're there, get some #12 barrel swivels. Don't bother getting expensive ones; the cheapest ones work fine.

Poke your leader through the swivel end of the snap swivel, and then tie on a barrel swivel. Now tie 2 to 3 ft. of tippet to the other end of the swivel. Your tippet should be about 1x or 2x, and Maxima tippet material is the first choice of steelheaders everywhere, because of its abrasion resistance.

Flies

The fly of choice is usually a glo-bug, an imitation of steelhead or salmon roe. Other flies will also work, like nymphs or wooly buggers, but none are as consistently productive as the good old glo-bug.

Drift-fishing works best where a fast-moving riffle meets the deeper water in a run. Strip off about 20 ft. of line, and have your slinky hanging about 8 ft. down from your rod tip.

Cast by using the tip of the rod to pitch the weight of the slinky up and across from your position. The weight of the slinky will quickly pull your fly to the bottom. Less weight is better than more, so your slinky doesn't drag over the rocks. Follow the path of your fly with

Drift-fishing Rig

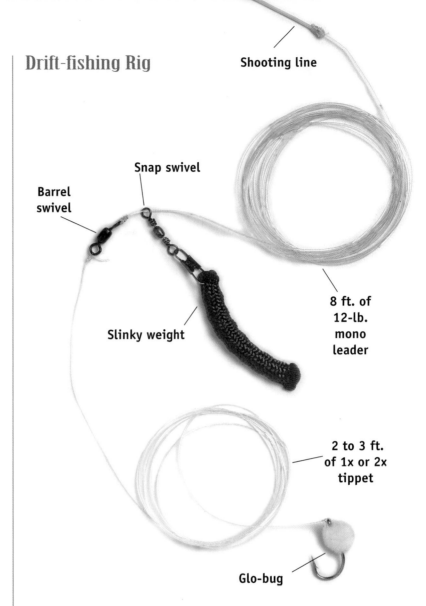

Shooting line

Snap swivel

Barrel swivel

Slinky weight

8 ft. of 12-lb. mono leader

2 to 3 ft. of 1x or 2x tippet

Glo-bug

the rod, as you feel the slinky just lightly tick over the rocky bottom.

When a steelhead takes your fly, it can feel like anything from a good yank to a slight hesitation in your drift. I've said it before, but now more than ever, when in doubt, set the hook! You will set the hook many times into rocks or other snags between actual strikes. If you're not getting snagged occasionally, you're probably not using enough weight. Put on a bigger slinky.

After drifting your fly through its original drift another five or six times, pull another 2 ft. of line off your reel, and

make another half-dozen drifts. Repeat until you are either drifting the far side of the current, or are at your maximum casting range. Now, take a couple of steps downstream and repeat the process.

When you get snagged (and you will), point your rod tip at the snag and pull with the line to free it or break it off. When you're using a slinky, it's almost always the fly that gets snagged. Since glo-bugs are cheap, don't worry if you go through a dozen or so in a day.

If you get your fly back off a snag, check the hook point. If it is even slightly dull, sharpen it or replace it.

Down-and-across Fishing

Several years ago, I started using Mepps-style spinners on a spinning rod. Most of the steelhead fishing I had done up until that time involved some kind of drift-fishing technique. Spinner fishing appealed to me because I liked the idea of covering water, and searching for aggressive fish.

Each day I fished, I covered every square foot of a section of river. I soon found that there was a pattern in where I got most of my strikes. I also found that a hot steelhead will chase down and strike something that invades its space, looks like food, or just irritates it.

I don't spinner fish for steelhead much anymore. I gave it up mostly because I decided that any steelhead that would chase down a spinner would chase down the right fly just as well.

I would always rather catch a fish on a fly rod than on a spinning rod, so I just had to apply what I learned from catching fish on a spinner to catching them on a fly.

The most important thing that I learned from spinner fishing was that all of the strikes I got occurred when I was fishing from the bottom half of a pool, down through the flat, and all the way to the tailout.

Technique

When I started to target these spinner-eating steelies with a fly, I concentrated on the same areas. Most of what I knew about West Coast fly fishing for steelhead involved using a down-and-across presentation with an 8-weight fly rod, rigged up with a sink-tip line. A short, 4-ft. leader went on the end of my line, and for a fly, I decided a big, black bunny leech should work as well as anything.

My technique was to cast the sink-tip across the stream, make a big mend to get the fly down a few feet, and then just let it swing in the current until it was below me. Make a cast, let it swing, and then take a step down. Hey, this is just like how

I fish streamers for trout! One thing I immediately liked about fishing this way was that I rarely got snagged.

The thing I liked best about using the down-and-across presentation, though, was that it worked! When a steelhead hits a swinging fly there is no mistaking it; when your rod tip gets violently jerked to the surface of the water you can be pretty sure that the fish didn't like your fly invading its space.

Just as when you are fishing any subsurface presentation, you have to visualize where your fly is at all times. Also try to get a feel for how deep it is riding. You don't need, or want, your fly to be right on the bottom, but just over the heads of the steelhead. The clearer the water, the higher your fly can be riding.

In water that is very clear, or when fish are very aggressive, you can use a floating line instead of a sink-tip. If you do use a floating line, a longer 9-ft. leader should be used, and a weighted fly should go on the end. Additional weight in the form of split shot can be put on the leader to help get the fly down.

Whether using a floating or sinking line, be sure to cover lots of water when fishing with a down-and across presentation. You are looking for aggressive fish. Make a cast, take a step down, and repeat. Keep moving!

Flies

Steelhead flies come in all sizes, shapes, and colors. When I started steelhead fishing, I enjoyed tying and fishing with many of the different patterns. I still have a box full of them, and I do use them occasionally. Most of the flies I use today, though, are variations on wooly

Wooly Bugger

Bunny Leech

buggers and bunny leeches.

It is rare to fish for steelhead and hook into enough fish in a day to determine if one fly really works better than others. In a typical day, you might fish for eight hours, and change flies periodically throughout the day. Why was the fish suddenly willing to bite—was it your fly, or was it that the fish was just ready to eat?

No one will ever know for sure, but using a reasonable fly, having confidence in it, and keeping it in the water are keys to success.

Nymph Fishing

Nymph fishing for steelhead has become more popular in recent years. Many anglers who have mainly fished for trout in the past are expanding their horizons, as well as the length of their fishing seasons, by pursuing steelhead. Since almost all trout anglers are familiar with nymph-fishing techniques that work for trout, these are often the techniques that novice steelheaders start with.

Technique

To rig up for nymph fishing for steelhead, you can use the same principles as with nymph fishing for trout: a weighted nymph, some extra weight above the tippet, and a strike indicator up near the tip of the floating fly line.

Nymphing is most effective in fast-moving riffles and runs. Make your casts upstream, or up-and-across-stream, and pay special attention to the edges or current seams. Steelhead often rest in the slow water that is adjacent to fast water.

Unlike other styles of steelheading, nymphing requires that you fish slowly and thoroughly, often making as many as ten or twenty casts to the same spot. Most strikes from steelhead are due to aggression or territoriality, but nymphing can bring a strike that is either due to actual feeding or the memory of eating nymphs as a youngster and it struck out of reflex. Either way, it works.

Flies

A wide variety of different nymphs will take steelhead. Stoneflies, hare's ears, princes, even caddis larva bring strikes. As always, exactly what fly you're using isn't as important as fishing in the right spot and having confidence in the fly. I'm amazed at how many steelhead are hooked and landed on flies that I would consider to be too small. Most nymphs used for steelhead are between size 6 and 10, but smaller ones can be successful, too.

Giant Black Stonefly Nymph

Prince Nymph

AFTERWORD

I fish a lot. Really, a lot. I have a garage full of rods, including many fly rods, but quite a few of them are spinning and bait-casting rods. I fish for all kinds of fish in all kinds of ways.

In fact, last weekend, I was in Florida to make still another attempt at catching a tarpon on a fly. No tarpon, but I did catch a few snook. Last night I fished in a fifty-boat bass tournament. My fishing partner and I caught our limit of five bass that ended up weighing just over 16 lbs. A pretty good bag of fish, but not good enough to make the money, since tenth place was over 17 lbs. There were no fly rods at all involved last night.

I just returned this evening from an outing with two friends. We fished on a stream that I have fished most of my life. As far as the actual catching went, well, let's say that it was a little slow. The stream looked good, and the air smelled great, though, and we did catch a few trout. Tomorrow, I'll be fishing for smallmouth bass, and next week muskies will be the target.

Am I spreading myself too thin? No, never! Not when it comes to fishing, and especially fly fishing.

In my work at a tackle shop, I talk to all types of anglers. Many are very versatile, catching many kinds of fish by a variety of methods. Most of today's best fly fishermen—guys like Lefty Kreh, Larry Dahlberg, Jose Wejebe, and Flip Pallot—are just as adept with a spinning or casting rod as they are with a fly rod.

I've always thought that fishing with all types of tackle for a variety of fish enables an angler to see "the big picture." Every style of fishing is related to every other style of fishing.

I caught hundreds of trout on worms, and quite a few on Mepps spinners, before I ever caught one on a fly. In the process of catching trout on non–fly-fishing gear, I learned much about how to catch them on flies later. I learned where trout live, and how their activity level and location are affected by weather and water levels. Some spots on the stream I fished as a kid (and still fish today) consistently produced larger trout than others. The knowledge that I gained by catching so many trout on bait and spinning tackle could not be learned from any magazine article or Saturday morning cable fishing show.

I'm lucky in that I was brought up fishing with a variety of different kinds of fishing tackle. I never thought that fishing with a fly rod was much different than fishing with any other kind of tackle—just a lot more fun, and sometimes more effective.

So if you've had experience with other types of fishing, great! If not, fly fishing can become your first fishing love.

A few things in this book may contradict some popular beliefs and theories on fly fishing. That doesn't mean that someone else's ideas are wrong, and I'm right. In most fly-fishing situations, there are at least several different ways to catch fish effectively. In this book, I've discussed what I think are the best and easiest ways to catch fish with a fly rod.

There are countless other books and magazine articles devoted to many of the individual topics I've touched on here. So after you've mastered these basics—and want to hone your skills—there will be plenty of new equipment, techniques, and locations to try.

As I said at the beginning of this book, it was fly fishing for trout that really started my love of fishing. And after 25 years I still love it. I hope you enjoy it for even longer!

FISHING GUIDES

My personal guiding experience began with a job at Camp Fish, a summer camp for kids who really loved to fish. As a fishing instructor, I took the kids out fishing in the mornings and in the evenings. We fished mostly for bass, panfish, and pike, but occasionally we went after muskies or trout. Afternoons were for fishing seminars given by myself and other instructors and counselors. What I learned about fishing during those summers—from both other instructors and the campers—has become invaluable to me.

I also worked for a couple of summers in Alaska at Tikchik Narrows Lodge. At Camp Fish, the people in my boat were usually happy catching a few sunnies or crappies. But this was a whole new ballgame! These people had paid thousands of dollars for a week, and they wanted to catch fish—big fish, and lots of them. The fishing up there was somewhat different than guiding on lakes and rivers for rainbow trout, grayling, salmon, lake trout, and char. But the skills I had learned by fishing for a wide variety of fish back home paid off, and I was able to consistently put my people on fish, even on water I had never seen before.

In recent years, I've been spending a fair amount of time guiding anglers on waters closer to home—mostly for smallmouth bass on the upper Mississippi River. The section of river that I fish the most is shallow, fast, and rocky. Some days, the smallies seem to be everywhere; other days, the river seems almost devoid of fish. Invariably, the days when the fish just aren't coming up for flies are the days when I have a good fly caster out with me. I don't know what's more frustrating, having a good caster out on a day when the fish are uncooperative, or having someone who just can't cast when the fish are really active.

It took me several years of guiding before I really got used to the idea of having other anglers catch the fish. I now enjoy watching other anglers catch fish under my instruction more than catching them myself. It's like taking angling to a higher level, getting anglers who are often beginners to cast where the fish are, to set the hook, to play the fish properly. If you're being guided by me, I want you to catch fish even more than you want to catch them.

Hiring a guide, however, does not guarantee that you will catch fish. There have been days when my clients, through no fault of theirs or mine, couldn't get bit. Some days, the fish just don't cooperate. I used to experience extremely high levels of stress when this happened. After all, these people were paying me to put them on fish. I've also had guides take me out, and

no fish were caught. In those situations, I still learn a lot about fishing unfamiliar waters. I learn the locations that have been productive in the past, what kinds of flies are usually productive, and general technique.

On occasion, your guide may want you to fish in a way or in a location that seems strange. In that case, a good rule of thumb is: When in doubt, listen to the guide! He or she wants you to catch fish and will give you his or her best advice.

Depending on where you go, the price of a guide will range from $200 to $400 for a full day, which is usually around eight hours. That may seem like a lot of money to spend for a day of fishing, but let me assure you that no one is getting rich by being a fishing guide. If a guide charges $300 a day, and books 100 days in a year, that's $30,000, before expenses. A long ways from getting rich. Spend $300 on a lawyer or dentist, and then let me know how much fun you had. A good guide knows his or her home waters intimately, and will take a lot of the guesswork out of it for you—like which locations are best for the conditions, and what flies are appropriate.

It's still up to you to make the cast, set the hook, and play the fish. But I firmly believe that you can easily learn more from one day with a guide than you could learn in a year on your own. Getting a guide is as close to a short-cut as there is in becoming a good fly angler.

Choosing a Guide

Here are a few tips and questions to ask when you're looking for a guide:

• Get references from people who have hired the guide in the past—friends, relatives, and co-workers make good sources of information.

• A good guide, like any other fishing partner, should be fun to be around. If possible, have a couple get-to-know-you conversations with the guide before you hire him or her.

• Make it clear what your expectations are, and what kind of fishing experience you want to have. You may be most interested in learning good locations on water close to home. You may want to just go out and catch a lot of fish, or maybe you want to target big fish.

• Be sure to let the guide know what your skill level is. The game plan can vary depending on the skill level of the angler.

• Find out what is provided by the guide—tackle, flies, lunch, drinks, etc. Most guides would just as soon have you use their equipment and flies. That way, they know that everything will be set up the way they like it.

FURTHER READING

A River Runs Through It and Other Stories
  by Norman MacLean, E. Annie Proulx
  2001 (25th Anniversary Edition),
  University of Chicago Press

Aquatic Entomology
  by W. Patrick McCafferty
  1983, Jones and Bartlett Publishing

Bluegill: Fly Fishing and Flies
  by Terry and Roxanne Wilson
  1999, Frank Amato Publications

Caddisflies
  by Gary Lafontaine
  1994, The Lyons Press

Dry Fly Fishing
  by Dave Hughes
  1994, Frank Amato Publications

Essence of Fly Casting
  (Volume I and Volume II video)
  by Mel Krieger

Essential Trout Flies
  by Dave Hughes
  2000, Stackpole Books

Everyone's Illustrated Guide to Trout on the Fly
  by R. Chris Halla
  1997, Frank Amato Publications

Fly Fishing Made Easy (Volume II video)
  by Brian and Judith O'Keefe

Fly Tying Made Clear and Simple
  by Skip Morris
  1992 Frank Amato Publications

Hatches II: Twentieth Anniversary Edition
  by Al Caucci and Bob Nastasi
  1995, The Lyons Press

Lefty's Little Fly-Fishing Tips
  by Left Kreh
  2002, The Lyons Press

Longer Fly Casting
  by Lefty Kreh
  1991, The Lyons Press

Matching Mayflies: Everything You Need to Know
to Match Any Mayfly You'll Ever Encounter
  by Dave Hughes
  2001, Frank Amato Publications

No Hatch to Match: Aggressive Strategies for
Fly-Fishing Between Hatches
  by Rich Osthoff
  2002, Stackpole Books

Nymph Fishing
  by Dave Hughes
  1995, Frank Amato Publications

Practical Knots II
  by Mark Sosin and Lefty Kreh
  1991, The Lyons Press

Presenting the Fly
  by Lefty Kreh
  1999, The Lyons Press

Smallmouth Strategies for the Fly Rod
  by Will Ryan
  1996, The Lyons Press

Snowfly: A Novel
  by Joseph Heywood
  2000, The Lyons Press

Steelhead Dreams: The Theory, Method, Science and
Madness of Great Lakes Steelhead Fly Fishing
  by Matt Supinski
  2001, Frank Amato Publications

Steelhead: Fly Fishing
  by Trey Combs
  1999, The Lyons Press

The River Why
  by David James Duncan
  2002, University of California Press

INDEX

PHOTO CREDITS

(Note: T=Top, C=Center, B=Bottom, L=Left, R=Right)

Creative Publishing international is the most complete source of How-To Information for the Outdoorsman

THE COMPLETE HUNTER™ Series

- *Advanced Whitetail Hunting*
- *America's Favorite Wild Game Recipes*
- *Bowhunting Equipment & Skills*
- *The Complete Guide to Hunting*
- *Cooking Wild in Kate's Kitchen*
- *Dressing & Cooking Wild Game*
- *Duck Hunting*
- *Elk Hunting*
- *Game Bird Cookery*
- *Hunting Record-Book Bucks*
- *Mule Deer Hunting*
- *Muzzleloading*
- *Pronghorn Hunting*
- *Venison Cookery*
- *Whitetail Deer*
- *Whitetail Techniques & Tactics*
- *Wild Turkey*

The Freshwater Angler™ Series

- *Advanced Bass Fishing*
- *All-Time Favorite Fish Recipes*
- *The Art of Fly Tying*
- *The Art of Freshwater Fishing*
- *The Complete Guide to Freshwater Fishing*
- *Fishing for Catfish*
- *Fishing Rivers & Streams*
- *Fishing Tips & Tricks*
- *Fishing With Artificial Lures*
- *Fly Fishing for Trout in Streams*
- *Largemouth Bass*
- *Modern Methods of Ice Fishing*
- *The New Cleaning & Cooking Fish*
- *Northern Pike & Muskie*
- *Panfish*
- *Smallmouth Bass*
- *Successful Walleye Fishing*
- *Trout*

The Complete FLY FISHERMAN™ Series

- *Fishing Dry Flies – Surface Presentations for Trout in Streams*
- *Fishing Nymphs, Wet Flies & Streamers – Subsurface Techniques for Trout in Streams*
- *Fly-Fishing Equipment & Skills*
- *Fly-Tying Techniques & Patterns*

*To purchase these or other titles, contact your local bookseller, or visit our web site at **www.creativepub.com**.*